QUALITY MANAGEMENT IN THE SERVICE INDUSTRY

ELLIS HORWOOD SERIES IN
APPLIED SCIENCE AND INDUSTRIAL TECHNOLOGY

Series Editor: Dr D. H. SHARP, OBE, former General Secretary, Society of Chemical Industry; formerly General Secretary, Institution of Chemical Engineers; and former Technical Director, Confederation of British Industry.

This collection of books is designed to meet the needs of technologists already working in fields to be covered, and for those new to the industries concerned. The series comprises valuable works of reference for scientists and engineers in many fields, with special usefulness to technologists and entrepreneurs in developing countries.

Students of chemical engineering, industrial and applied chemistry, and related fields, will also find these books of great use, with their emphasis on the practical technology as well as theory. The authors are highly qualified chemical engineers and industrial chemists with extensive experience, who write with the authority gained from their years in industry.

Published and in active publication

PRACTICAL USES OF DIAMONDS
A. BAKON, Research Centre of Geological Technique, Warsaw, and A. SZYMANSKI, Institute of Electronic Materials Technology, Warsaw
NATURAL GLASSES
V. BOUSKA, *et al.*, Czechoslovak Society for Mineralogy & Geology, Czechoslovakia
POTTERY SCIENCE: Materials, Processes and Products
A. DINSDALE, lately Director of Research, British Ceramic Research Association
MATCHMAKING: Science, Technology and Manufacture
C. A. FINCH, Managing Director, Pentafin Associates, Chemical, Technical and Media Consultants, Stoke Mandeville, and S. RAMACHANDRAN, Senior Consultant, United Nations Industrial Development Organisation for the Match Industry
THE HOSPITAL LABORATORY: Strategy, Equipment, Management and Economics
T. B. HALES, Arrowe Park Hospital, Merseyside
OFFSHORE PETROLEUM TECHNOLOGY AND DRILLING EQUIPMENT
R. HOSIE, formerly of Robert Gordon's Institute of Technology, Aberdeen
MEASURING COLOUR
R. W. G. HUNT, Visiting Professor, The City University, London
MODERN APPLIED ENERGY CONSERVATION
Editor: K. JACQUES, University of Stirling, Scotland
CHARACTERIZATION OF FOSSIL FUEL LIQUIDS
D. W. JONES, University of Bristol
PAINT AND SURFACE COATINGS: Theory and Practice
Editor: R. LAMBOURNE, Technical Manager, INDCOLLAG (Industrial Colloid Advisory Group), Department of Physical Chemistry, University of Bristol
CROP PROTECTION CHEMICALS
B. G. LEVER, Development Manager, ICI plc Plant Protection Division
HANDBOOK OF MATERIALS HANDLING
Translated by R. G. T. LINDKVIST, MTG, Translation Editor: R. ROBINSON, Editor, *Materials Handling News*. Technical Editor: G. LUNDESJO, Rolatruc Limited
FERTILIZER TECHNOLOGY
G. C. LOWRISON, Consultant, Bradford
NON-WOVEN BONDED FABRICS
Editor: J. LUNENSCHLOSS, Institute of Textile Technology of the Rhenish-Westphalian Technical University, Aachen, and W. ALBRECHT, Wuppertal
PROFIT BY QUALITY: The Essentials of Industrial Survival
P. W. MOIR, Consultant, West Sussex
EFFICIENT BEYOND IMAGINING: CIM and Its Applications for Today's Industry
P. W. MOIR, Consultant, West Sussex
TRANSIENT SIMULATION METHODS FOR GAS NETWORKS
A. J. OSIADACZ, UMIST, Manchester

Series continued at back of book

QUALITY MANAGEMENT IN THE SERVICE INDUSTRY

LIONEL STEBBING FIQA, FAQMC, SMASQC
Senior Partner and Principal Consultant
Stebbing and Partners International

ELLIS HORWOOD
NEW YORK   LONDON   TORONTO   SYDNEY   TOKYO   SINGAPORE

First published in 1990 by
ELLIS HORWOOD LIMITED
Market Cross House, Cooper Street,
Chichester, West Sussex, PO19 1EB, England

A division of
Simon & Schuster International Group
A Paramount Communications Company

Typeset by Ellis Horwood Limited
Printed and bound in Great Britain
by Bookcraft (Bath) Limited, Midsomer Norton, Avon

British Library Cataloguing in Publication Data

Stebbing, Lionel
Quality management in the service industry
CIP catalogue record for this book is available from the British Library
ISBN 0–13–747148–3

Library of Congress Cataloging-in-Publication Data available

He profits most who serves best.

[Motto for international rotary]
A. F. Sheldon

Table of contents

Table of contents

Preface

Diseases desperate grown, by desperate appliance are relieved, or not at all.

William Shakespeare, *Hamlet.*

The excellent reception given to my first book *Quality assurance: the route to efficiency and competitiveness* has resulted in many requests world-wide for a book on the same subject but specifically addressing service organizations.

Quality management originated in the manufacturing industry and therefore most of the techniques were manufacturing orientated. I have found that applying similar techniques to service organizations has met with great success as the concepts, principles and practices of quality management are appropriate to any type of industry and to any type of company. It is simply a matter of thoughtful adaptation.

In the final analysis, failure to meet customer needs and expectations can have far reaching consequences that may have an adverse affect on both the customer and the service organization alike. It is the responsibility of management, therefore, to ensure that such failures are prevented and, in the event of failure, to implement speedy corrective action and action to prevent a recurrence of such failure. This is what quality management is all about!

As there are so many parallels which can be drawn between the service industry and the manufacturing industry with regard to quality management concepts, I have had great difficulty in not repeating what I have already covered in my previous book but, inevitably, I have had to do so in some instances. These instances refer particularly to the quality audit, quality circles and the management review. Those who are in possession of my first book will find some duplication but I trust this will not detract from the message I give here.

Lionel Stebbing

August 1990

Acknowledgements

The author wishes to acknowledge assistance and co-operation with the supply of information from:

British Standards Institution
Department of Trade and Industry
Institute of Quality Assurance
National Society of Quality Circles
Standards Australia

My grateful appreciation, as for my first book, must once again be given to my wife Betty who has assisted me with the development of the manuscript and without whose encouragement I would never have completed it.

Thanks are also due to Dr David Sharp OBE, Series Editor, for his valuable advice and assistance throughout the whole of this project.

Introduction

The bearings of this observation lays in the application on it.
Charles Dickens, *Dombey and Son.*

The Industrial Revolution in England, which began about 1760, resulted in the replacement of the domestic system of manufacturing by the factory system, in other words progress from manual to machine techniques.

This transfer to machine techniques brought with it a number of problems, particularly that associated with controlling the manufacturing process, and thus the need to control manufacturing activities. This saw the birth of inspection techniques.

We have, naturally, come a long way since then, with the war years adding greatly to a much firmer control of the design and manufacture of armaments and later with the nuclear industry augmenting these controls in order to comply with much greater safety requirements.

The military and nuclear industries have been implementing quality systems for many years now and it is only since the 1970s that attention has been given to implementing similar systems into general manufacturing activities. The 1970s also saw major improvements in manufacturing efficiency through the utilization of automation and enhanced management techniques.

The 1980s saw attention directed towards design and marketing as a method of achieving a competitive advantage and this has had a tremendous impact on the ability of many large organizations such as American Express, GEC Plessey, IBM, ICL, Philips, Proctor and Gamble, Rank Xerox, and others to stay 'ahead of the game'. Those organizations which have invested in quality management will continue to thrive and the author is of the opinion that all organizations, large and small alike, whether engaged in giving a service or manufacturing a product, must follow the example of those companies which have introduced quality management and are reaping the benefits of their decision to do so.

There are many challenges awaiting management in the 1990s, not least of which will be the necessity to manage change. It is impossible to remain static in business and in today's business environment external factors are having such an impact and are moving at such a tremendous pace that the ability to react to the needs of a dynamic market-place must be paramount as a means of business survival.

The requirement for change is being driven by a number of issues, not the least of which are:

— the opening up of hitherto restricted markets;
— the increasing needs and expectations of customers, for both services and products alike;
— the ability to respond to changes in demand for services and products with short delivery times.

These are reasons enough for executives to look to quality management as an issue which must be addressed if their companies are to remain efficient and profitable in what is an increasingly competitive market-place.

It is important, therefore, when setting out on the long journey of quality management that, initially, one must identify:

— the customers' requirements — their needs and expectations, so to speak
— the company's own strengths and weaknesses
— the strengths and weaknesses of the competition.

In other words we must ask ourselves four questions:

(1) where are we now?
(2) where do we want to get to and by when?
(3) how do we get there?
(4) and once having got there — what is the next step?

Establishing 'where we are now' is probably the easiest part of the exercise. The answers to the other questions can be achieved only by the determined effort and commitment of top management and by the adoption of quality management techniques. Objectives must be clearly established and defined and all in the company must be able to relate to them. This will probably mean a complete change in attitude from the whole work-force.

Quality management is not all about checking or after-the-event control activities, it is about leadership and setting the standards for work and achievement and, above all, team work.

Quality management is a different way for an organization to think and act. It forces companies to look outward rather than inward and this can be difficult, especially for large organizations where power has been held at the centre and also where the customer has been treated with casual indifference, as is the case with some public sector industries.

The general principles and practices of quality management are appropriate to all organizations, large or small, regardless of the product or service and, although a small organization will not have, nor will it require, the multifarious structure of the larger organization, the same considerations for the management of quality still apply.

In the development of any quality management system it must be borne in mind, however, that the system must be tailored to suit the size and complexity of the organization concerned. For example, if a simple checklist will suffice instead of a detailed narrative document, then use it. The difference is simply one of scale and application. In other words — *make the system work for you, not you for the system.*

Bearing in mind this premise, if this book answers the four questions posed above, it will have served its purpose.

Quality management

PROFITABILITY AND EFFICIENCY

Assume a virtue, if you have it not.

William Shakespeare, *Hamlet.*

Quality management is the managing of all functions and activities necessary to determine and achieve quality. As such, quality management probably offers more scope for achieving and maintaining a company's competitive advantage than many other management techniques. In pragmatic terms this means providing a product, or service, which is satisfactory to the customer at a price commensurate with that satisfaction (i.e. value for money), in the most cost effective and efficient manner. In other words, maximizing profitability and efficiency in a competitive market-place.

THE SERVICE INDUSTRY

It is not generally appreciated that in most industrialized nations at least 65% of the total work force is involved in what could be termed 'the service industry', the service industry being that section of the economy which supplies the needs of the consumer but produces no tangible goods. We all use and depend on services in one form or another and, generally, the quality of the services given can add much to the quality of life. In the main, the largest constituents of this total relate to finance (including banking, insurance, building societies), travel, health care, public utilities, education, local government, hotels, restaurants and the retail trade. All of these supply a need to the customer, yet, in very few cases is this need, which in itself is a product, considered in the light of quality.

It is worth pointing out at this juncture that, in the service industry, actual prices charged are often of secondary importance. For example, a customer will choose a 'good' restaurant because of the ambience, service and quality of the food. People are quite prepared to pay for this provided they get what they regard as value for money.

It could be argued that health care, public utilities and the like should not be seen as profit-making organizations but nevertheless the service offered by them should satisfy the customer and should be reasonably priced (value for money). Although, in many instances, such service organizations are not operating in a competitive environment, the customer will expect satisfaction and efficiency of service.

MANAGEMENT OF QUALITY

Quality, to most people, is associated with a tangible item and is not totally recognized as being a 'people-based' attribute. Quality management *per se* is, therefore, generally seen as being hardware-related and limited in application only to engineering and manufacturing activities. In addition, many large organizations see quality management as being good for their suppliers to implement but not necessarily relevant to their own activities. This is particularly so in relation to what we term the 'service industry'.

Much of the confusion, or lack of acceptance, which presently exists is probably due to the word *quality*, which in the context of quality management has a precise meaning:

> *The totality of features and characteristics of a product or service that bear upon its ability to satisfy stated or implied needs.*
> *(ISO 8402 - 1986: Quality — vocabulary)*

It is to be noted that this definition includes services.
The ability to manage quality, therefore, must be based on stated or implied needs. The requirements of the customer must be totally understood if the service is to satisfy that need.

CUSTOMER REQUIREMENTS — STATED OR IMPLIED

In terms of identifying the need, externally this will be determined by the customer either specifying the need by means of a written description (the stated need) or by means of market research and general understanding (the implied need). Internally this can be seen as supplying the service, or the product of one's endeavours, to the stated need. In this internal sense the stated need will be in the form of the documented work instructions. The subject of work instructions will be dealt with in detail in Chapter 6.

In terms of understanding, perhaps George Bernard Shaw's description of quality could well be suited to the service industry. He wrote in his play *John Bull's Other Island*:

There are only two qualities in this world, efficiency and inefficiency; and only two sorts of people, the efficient and the inefficient.

There is a great deal of truth in that statement. Efficiency is what every senior executive should be striving for and efficiency in service is what every customer is expecting. Inefficiency is usually the result of insufficient or inadequate training, or the person is unsuited for the task being undertaken. In both cases management has not identified the problem.

As far as the customer is concerned, efficiency in service could well be broken down into a number of attributes.

THE ATTRIBUTES OF EFFICIENCY

In his previous book *Quality assurance: the route to efficiency and competitiveness*, the author called up the eight C's of the total presentation of quality assurance. In the present context, these attributes could well be expanded to 12 C's:

Commitment
Consistency
Competence
Contact
Communication
Credibility
Compassion
Courtesy
Co-operation
Capability
Confidence
Criticism

Taking each in turn:

Commitment
The service organization commits itself to providing a service of some kind and a business is developed on that basis. Management should also commit itself to producing that service in the most efficient and profitable manner. Such commitment will manifest itself internally in the form of a quality

management system, which will encompass all aspects of the business. Quality management applies to the whole business activity and not just to the product or the service.

Consistency

The offered service should be consistent in performance and should be dependable. The organization will honour its commitment to the customer and will perform the service right first time.

Much the same philosophy applies internally within the workplace at each stage of the business. The customer may be regarded as the next stage in the process. However, internally, rather than a customer–supplier relationship, this could be termed a receiver–producer relationship. The internal service should be consistent and dependable. To use a cliché, we should all get it right first time every time. In this context 'it' can be anything: typing a letter, entering a figure on a balance sheet, issuing an invoice, producing a legal brief, cleaning a window, treating a patient, repairing a washing machine, installing a telephone, cleaning a hotel room, serving a customer in a restaurant, and so on. What must be first established is what 'it' is, how important 'it' is and how best to achieve 'it' in the most effective and efficient manner.

Competence

The organization will possess personnel with the required skills, knowledge and competence to perform the service. No organization can expect to engage staff who will understand the working methods of a company immediately. Inherent in competency must be some form of training: training internally to serve the company well and training in an external sense to satisfy the customer with the given service.

Contact

The organization will, or should, permit ease of contact by the customer to the correct personnel. Internally, the same philosophy should exist. Management should permit ease of contact by the work-force to the cognizant management representative.

Communication

The organization should be keeping the customer and the employees informed. Communication is, unfortunately, the most abused of the attributes.

Credibility

The organization should be worthy of belief. The organization has its customers' and its employees' best interests at heart.

Compassion
This is the ability to be sympathetic to a customer's needs. Internally, it is the ability of management to be sympathetic to an employee's needs.

Courtesy
Be polite, kind and considerate to the customer in manner or address. Again, this is implicit in employee relationships. Treat others as you would expect to be treated yourself.

Co-operation
Work together with the customer to the same end. Internally this would equally apply.

Capability
The organization should have the power of action to undertake the service being provided. This, in essence, goes hand in hand with competence in having the ability to undertake the assigned task.

Confidence
Achieve the confidence of the customer so that repeat business will result or recommendations made. Internally achieve the confidence of management and one's colleagues so that one's abilities are not questioned.

Criticism
Always take a critical approach to what one does: 'that will do' will never do! Encourage self-criticism. Invite constructive criticism from one's customers (in both the internal and external situations) and act upon it.

Additionally there is one further 'C' which applies mainly in the external sense and that is **Competition**. One must always be aware of the competition and beat it.

THE TOTALITY OF QUALITY MANAGEMENT

Quality management will, in order to achieve the 12 attributes as described above, include in its totality a continuous cycle of planning, training, actioning, monitoring, improving and reviewing the performance of an organization. In short: P-T-A-M-I-R, Plan, Train, Action Monitor, Improve, Review. These are summed up in the 'Quality management wheel' (see Fig. 1.1). Each of these aspects will be dealt with in detail in the following chapters.

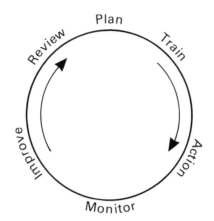

Fig. 1.1 — The quality management wheel.

2

Internal inveterate waste

How use doth breed habit in a man.
William Shakespeare, *The two gentlemen of Verona.*

POOR PERFORMANCE

Experience has shown that, regardless of the type or nature of a business, there is an element of expenditure relating to avoidable mistakes, waste, inefficiencies and poor performance. This expenditure could be described as inveterate waste. It is habitual and organizations have accepted it as part of their operating costs. Nothing has been done to reduce or eliminate it. The end result is that the cost of this waste is built into the cost of providing the service.

Many companies, when developing a budget for a given job, simply add on a percentage to cover this waste. 'Plus ten per cent for the hassle factor' so to speak. There is no system to identify the scale of this waste.

It is worthwhile looking into these areas. The following is not an exhaustive list but it does represent a typical range applicable to most companies:

— duplication of activities
— redoing incorrect work
— unnecessary inspection
— scrapped work (letters, invoices, etc.)

— unnecessary distribution of documentation.

For example, how many times is one confronted with the statement 'no problems — if I make a mistake someone else will catch it'. In this instance, there is the time involved initially to produce the mistake, the time taken to discover it and then the time taken to redo the work, plus the cost of the consumable — be it a letter, invoice, purchase order, and so on. There is a multiplying factor in not getting it right first time. In addition, one may experience costs in dealing with the complaints from customers which emanate from these errors.

COST ESCALATION

Let us examine how such costs can escalate. For example, an invoice for services rendered could contain an error. This invoice is received by the customer, who identifies the error and returns the invoice for rectification. The invoice is amended and returned to the customer for payment. The time taken to rectify the error could amount to many weeks. Cash flow is halted and, in the case of sizeable sums, it may be necessary for the supplier to support this delay in payment by obtaining credit at considerable interest. In the case of small companies, where cash flow is extremely important, delays in invoice payments can cause serious difficulties and, in some cases, have been known to lead to bankruptcy.

Unnecessary distribution of documents is another wasteful exercise. It is on record that twenty to eighty times the unit cost spent on producing documents is spent in processing, copying, distributing, filing and eventually destroying them. In most companies employees maintain their own series of documents which could be adequately maintained by a central source. There is generally no systematic control over document production and distribution.

In essence then, the typical list of wasted areas given earlier, when examined in detail, would escalate and the list would expand to include:

— errors;
— cost of making errors and redoing the work;
— scrap;
— cost of producing the scrap;
— cost of inspecting, rejecting and generally troubleshooting;
— cost of dealing with the resultant customer complaints and rectifying the problem;
— cost of possible liability claims;
— cost of loss of customer;

— interest on payments retained owing to the defective service;
— interest on incorrectly invoiced services;
— costs due to demotivation of e ployees.

THE COST OF NON-CONFORMANCE

What is not generally appreciated by many company executives is the enormity of the costs associated with the above. Surveys carried out in North America, Europe and Australia have shown that this inveterate waste can vary from 5% to 45% of a company's revenue. It is now generally accepted that within the majority of companies the range is between 15% and 30% of revenue. This means that, in many instances, the cost of inveterate waste can be greater than before-tax profits. In order to place this into some sort of perspective, it is worthwhile examining an actual case.

A company supplying manufactured products and services to a government agency was instructed, under the government's purchasing policy, to produce evidence of the implementation of an adequate management system. The company concerned was adamant that, as it received relatively few customer complaints and was making a reasonable profit — 12.37% of revenue — there was little need to implement any additional systems.

The author, however, was requested to examine the company's systems and to identify any shortcomings. Management, needless to say, were very sceptical of the outcome and could foresee nothing but additional cost and paperwork in meeting the customer's requirements. This is a typical reaction by most companies when faced with the imposition of quality management systems. It is seen as additional bureaucracy with no financial gain.

The author adopted the approach that all companies, regardless of size or product, have an element of inveterate waste and, in order to prove the point, required an example. The result of just one area of the assessment was quite revealing. It was ascertained that, owing to the lack of adequate in-house training schemes for new employees, considerable time was wasted during the first three weeks of employment in endeavouring to find out how the company operated.

For example, four new highly paid and highly qualified employees admitted that they had wasted considerable time getting to grips with the company's departmental routines. It was felt by each of them that, because they were highly qualified and highly paid, they should not be questioning how the company worked, so the first three weeks were very unproductive.

Three weeks salary down the drain. This one instance multiplied by the number of new employees taken on during the course of a year amounted to many thousands of pounds. In the one area of training alone, the company was experiencing considerable losses. Other areas where the company lacked management systems were:

— planning,
— document control,
— record-keeping,
— corrective action.

The end result was that inveterate waste was costing them in the region of 15% of revenue, 21% more than their pretax profit (2.6 percentage points of total revenue).

Let us put some figures to this waste. Revenue for the company in the year under discussion was £59 800 000. Operating profit amounted to £7 397 260. (12.37%). At the very best, owing to the lack of an adequate quality management system, it was ascertained that inveterate waste amounted to 15% of revenue or £8 970 000. Money down the drain! What was more staggering, however, is that with a total payroll of 900 personnel, when this figure was broken down on a cost per employee basis it worked out at £9966 per head per year, which, in many instances, amounted to more than a person's salary.

Of course, management had a hard time in believing such figures but at that time had no means to disprove them. They could not measure their quality costs. Can you?

Imposition by the government agency did, in effect, turn out to be a life-saver to this company. By developing and implementing quality systems, the company was able considerably to reduce its operating costs. These savings were used in a number of ways:

— to reduce the price of the product and thus stave off competition from overseas
— to increase reinvestment in new technology.

Additional bonuses were:

— an increase in the market share due to a cheaper product,
— enhanced shareholder dividends,
— improved employee morale,
— enhanced company image.

There are no miraculous cures to improve quality. One has to work hard at it, to commit cost, time and resources to it, to develop the management systems which suit that particular organization's requirements and then to monitor the application and effectiveness of the systems and amend, fine tune and train as necessary. It is a long, hard process but it is an investment that will pay great dividends if one keeps at it.

There is a growing tendency for organizations to seek immediate improvements by employing so called 'quality improvement techniques' such as quality circles, just in time (JIT), etc., without first establishing a base line from which to judge the overall effect of such 'improvements', in other words without developing the ability to measure quality costs.

There is also the conflict between the two philosophies of 'total quality control' (TQC) and 'quality management systems'. The former being dependent upon the statistical approach to problem-solving, whereas the latter sets out to develop and implement systems to control each activity, with the built-in mechanism to monitor the effect and application of the systems.

The author is an advocate of the latter, as without first establishing the systems and then monitoring or auditing them how can one be sure of the result? The statistical approach to problem-solving should come later as a tool for quality improvement, similarly, JIT, quality circles and such other improvement 'tools'.

Many of these quality improvement tools, in many instances, will not work. The small organizations of say five or six people struggling to keep their heads above water in the 'sea of competition', grasp such tools as a drowning man would grasp anything that floats, only to be disenchanted when it is found impractical for that particular company.

Just because a particular package — TQC, JIT, SPC, etc. — has been found to work in one particular organization, it does not follow that it will work elsewhere — particularly if the industry or service sector is different (i.e. manufacturing versus services).

There is no single proven cure. Like the doctor, the company must first diagnose the problem then establish a cure. That cure must treat the cause and not the symptom. It is, unfortunately, the symptom which is often treated.

It is disappointing to find that there still exists the same time-honoured excuses which seem to be prevalent in most of the world's industrialized nations. The most notable and often repeated being:

— I was going to call you but . . .
— Didn't you get my message?
— It will be delivered tomorrow.
— It's in the mail.
— Don't worry — we can change it.

Most of these excuses are the result of inefficient or non-existent management systems.

Surely it is not outside our capabilities to develop and implement systems which would alleviate these problems, then, having developed the systems, to build in the mechanism to make sure they are working properly and to review their effectiveness on a regular basis.

Most companies the author has consulted with, or talked to, in many countries do have systems which were developed years ago and never documented. It is generally assumed by management that the systems are still working even though times, people, and, in some cases, technology have changed.

If the customer does not complain — and most do not — management is unaware of the inefficiencies, duplications, short cuts and waste which have crept into the organization and with which the organization has learned to live. Nothing is done until the market share diminishes and profits dip below the acceptable. It is then, and only then, that most companies take action. In many instances it is too late.

In order to clarify this point let us assume, therefore, that point A in Fig. 2.1 is when management realizes that something must be done to halt this decline in its sales figures. Quality 'improvement' techniques are employed either using in-house resources or employing a consultant. In a short time there is noticeable 'improvement' and point B (Fig. 2.1) is reached.

Management is happy and the consultant (if one was used) is also happy. 'Improvement' in many instances is a misnomer. All that has happened in reality is to bring efficiency, or quality, or whatever one wishes to call it, back to where it was some time before.

All is well . . . for a time. Efficiency then drops off again as there is no management system to monitor the effect of, and continued application and implementation of, such 'improvement'. Efficiency will continue to dip until it reaches the same point where action was taken in the first instance. This time, however, action is usually delayed in the vain hope that it will right itself. After a while management will act again to bring efficiency back to where it was previously, and so it goes on until the customer takes action and refuses to buy the service or product, owing to its high price, erratic delivery, inferior performance or a combination of all three. The company then goes out of business! Fig. 2.1 shows the customer tolerance level remaining constant but, in actual fact, customers' requirements and expectations actually increase so, in reality, the customer tolerance level would take an upward curve.

What should happen is that the company sets its 'quality' target at an optimum level. This level will depend on the nature of the service or product and the way the company works. For example, a company manufacturing microwave ovens may well decide to set quality levels to achieve 999 satisfied customers out of 1000. To attempt to attain perfection at this stage would require very stringent control of all manufacturing processes, which could well double the price of the product and make it uncompetitive. Management must make this decision. On the other hand, if a company manufactures parachutes, then the controls must be set to achieve 100 per cent satisfaction!! Having established the 'level', then management must decide which of its activities are critical in achieving that 'level' and develop and implement systems (procedures) to control those activities.

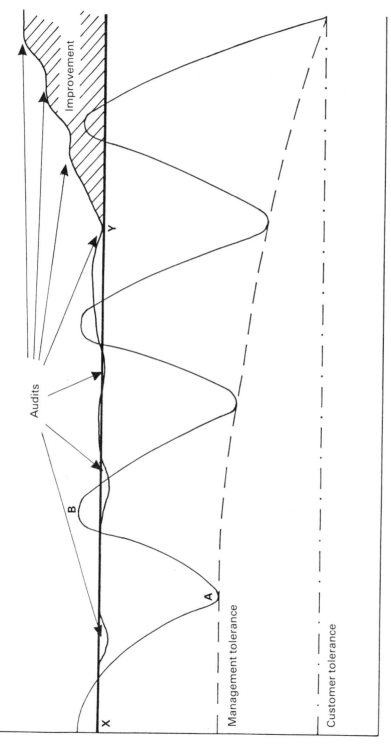

Fig. 2.1 — Quality level.

Let us assume that the 'quality level' has been set at point X on Fig. 2.1 — not quite as high as previously. Systems are developed and implemented which will mean an 'up-front' cost. A programme of audits is scheduled and it will be seen that in between audits (particularly during the early stages of implementation) efficiency or quality, or whatever name one wishes to give this attainment of customer satisfaction, may dip slightly. The audits will pick up deficiencies in the systems. These deficiencies may be due to lack of compliance or lack of training/awareness, or perhaps the system itself is wrong. Whatever the cause, corrective action must be taken to correct the deficiency and action taken to prevent a recurrence of the deficiency. Management must get involved in this action.

As time goes on, people become used to working in a controlled and regularly monitored environment. The systems become a way of life. Once this point is reached (Point Y on Fig, 2.1), then management can start thinking of ways to improve what is being done. This improvement can be looked upon in two aspects:

(1) to improve the way in which things are done;
(2) to improve the service or product, or perhaps a combination of both.

The achievement of such a position will involve money, time and very hard work but the dividends are tremendous if one keeps at it.

We shall now look at how the cost of inveterate waste can be identified, assessed and controlled.

3

Quality costs: identification, assessment and control

With affection beaming in one eye, and calculation shining out of the other.
Charles Dickens — *Martin Chuzzlewit.*

QUALITY COST DEFINITION

In general, most organizations do not measure quality costs explicitly since such costs are not required for the development of financial profit/loss statements, although they can have a significant affect on the profitability of a company. In the absence of a quality cost audit system it is extremely difficult for such organizations to determine effectively where such costs arise and how they can be controlled or reduced. Also, because there is no statutory requirement to collect and report on quality costs, the definitions of what constitutes a quality cost can be many and varied.

Generally, quality costs can be allocated to three distinct costing centres, as follows:

— prevention,
— appraisal (or inspection),
— failure/rectification.

It is worthwhile examining in detail how such costs are derived.
Quality costs can be defined as the difference between the actual total inclusive costs of carrying out a service, or manufacturing and selling an item, and the costs which would obtain if there had been no failure during any part

of the process. In other words, the costs associated with someone, somewhere, not getting it right first time.

It could be argued, however, that the costs of prevention and appraisal (inspection) are part of the total process costs and would be incurred in any event, which means that only the failure/rectification (and loss of future business) costs would be the difference between actual costs and those which would have been obtained if there had been no failures.

This argument could hold water if management has eliminated all unnecessary preventative and appraisal measures but, in a badly planned and managed situation, a good deal could be spent on prevention and appraisal yet still result in high failure/rectification. As quality becomes established, costs on prevention and appraisal should be minimized but a business must know what these costs are in order to achieve an optimum goal.

In setting up the quality management system (which will be discussed later), management will incur costs initially during the planning stage and later in the implementation, maintenance, review and improvement stages. The costs incurred in such instances would be construed as prevention costs, in other words, the allocation of the necessary resources to prevent failures from happening.

In any quality management system there always will be the requirement for checking or supervising some part of the process. Complicated activities will need, at some stage or other, to be reviewed or checked by a peer or supervisor in order to ascertain that the process has been carried out correctly. The identification of, and the requirement for, such reviews or checks will be a management decision which should be made during the planning and development stage of the quality system. There will ultimately, however, be costs incurred in carrying out these reviews and checks and these are known as appraisal costs.

Failure/rectification costs are those associated with failure to meet specified requirements and the resulting rectification or corrective action. These costs can be related to both internal and external activities: internal, where failure of some part of the process occurs *prior* to transfer to the customer, i.e. during the producer/receiver activity, and external, where there is a failure to conform to requirements *after* transfer to the customer.

In the service industry these costs would be as follows.

Prevention costs

These are incurred to reduce the costs associated with the failure, rectification and/or appraisal of the process and would normally be related to:

— the activities of planning and implementing the quality management system, developing the system documentation, checking and approving

such documentation, and distributing or communicating the information contained within the documentation;
— the activity involving the verification of the entire quality management system, i.e. the internal quality audit;
— the subsequent management review of the entire system;
— the assessment and verification of suppliers' organizations;
— the costs associated with training and education, which will include the development, implementation, operation and maintenance of in-house and external training programmes;
— the costs related to developing and implementing quality improvement programmes, such as quality circles, performance measurement; problem solving; statistical process control, and others.

Appraisal costs
These are the costs incurred in verifying the conformance of the process to requirements and would normally include the following:

— verifying that items received are in conformance with requirements (items can comprise a consignment of drugs, cleaning materials, stationery, or any other product associated with the running of one's business);
— checking and verifying the service activity throughout the process and then, finally, confirming the quality of the completed work. To give some examples, a check that an hotel room is clean and that the beds are properly made, a check of an invoice or letter prior to despatch, verification of the accuracy of a legal brief;
— analysis and reporting of verification results, which are conducted after confirming that the activity has been satisfactorily accomplished;
— the costs associated with the storage of records, such as customer records, patient care records, and others.

Failure/rectification costs
These are the costs associated with 'getting it wrong' and, subsequently 'putting it right'. Internally, these can include such things as scrap; corrective action; re-verification and downtime.

Failure costs can also arise externally when faults are discovered after transfer to the customer and will include such things as: the time spent in dealing with customer complaints; concessions; corrective action; liability claims. Intangible costs such as those associated with the loss of future sales and possible damage to the corporate image of the company should also be considered under this heading. Damage to the corporate image of a company can result in the loss of either individual customers or a failure to attract potential new customers, thus reducing the company's market share. Quality costs under this heading can be, at the very best, only an estimate but nevertheless they should be considered, as such costs could well amount to a considerable proportion of the total. Where such damage to a company's reputation does occur then, of course, corrective action must be taken to overcome it.

ESTABLISHING A QUALITY COST DATA BASE

Once having verified the costing areas, it will be necessary to establish a method of collecting, segregating and accounting for such costs. There are, therefore, a number of steps to be taken to achieve a satisfactory quality cost data base, as follows:

(1) Identify all quality cost activities.
(2) Segregate the activities into prevention, appraisal and failure/rectification.
(3) Establish a system to record the costs associated with prevention, appraisal and failure/rectification.
(4) Develop a suitable accounting system which will allocate the costs to the applicable activity and which will facilitate prompt retrieval of the information for regular review and analysis.

Let us take each in turn.

Identify all quality cost activities
This is a management exercise where a determination must be made of the means required to meet the objectives of the quality management system. Management must decide where supervision is required, including by whom; when and where a verification/inspection activity is to be carried out and by whom; what documentation is required to be checked and by whom; when internal quality audits are to be carried out and by whom.

At the end of the day the purpose of a quality management system should be to increase prevention and so reduce appraisal and failure/rectification activities.

Segregate the activities into prevention, appraisal and failure/rectification costs
This is as its title suggests. Having identified the who, how, what, when and where of a quality cost activity the decision should then be made to determine under which category each activity will be recorded. For example:

— Planning, process reviews, auditing, training, and quality improvement would fall under the category of prevention.
— Document checking and approval, receiving inspection, in-process and

final inspection, and record storage would fall under the category of appraisal.
— Scrap, corrective action, re-inspection, downtime, complaints, recall, warranty claims, public liability, and loss of future business would fall under the category of failure/rectification.

Establish a system to record the costs

This step will require the development of a reporting system which will accurately record time spent on quality cost activities *vis-à-vis* process activities. This may well mean establishing a time sheet recording method with suitable alphanumeric costing codes which will allot the activity to a specific cost centre, for example:

— suffix A to an action could indicate a prevention cost;
— suffix B, an appraisal cost;
— suffix C, a failure/rectification cost.

These codes could be subdivided to indicate a specific action within the cost centre category, for example:

Prevention
    — A1 could indicate quality management planning
    — A2, procedure development
    — A3, internal quality audits
    — A4, quality training

Appraisal
    — B1, supervision
    — B2, incoming inspection
    — B3, document checking and approval
    — B4, record storage

Failure/rectification
    — C1, scrap
    — C2, rectification
    — C3, customer complaints
    — C4, warranty claims

and so on.
    To put this in greater perspective and using a hypothetical situation, there could be an instance where an internal quality audit was carried out on a specific contract (the contract number being 89024) in which case the cost code would be:

89024-A3

or, perhaps, a document had to be revised due to a drafting error, in which case the cost code would be:

89024-C2

Whatever system is used, there will very probably be a requirement for management to promote an awareness campaign to put forward the benefits of such a costing system to the work force. There is the possibility of negative attitudes from some employees who may see time recording in such detail as a threat. This must not be allowed to happen as the co-operation of all concerned is imperative.

In the author's experience, most negative attitudes towards quality cost accounting emanate from upper and middle management who, in the past, have not had to record time expended on any particular task. In this respect an attitudinal change is paramount. The system developed must, therefore, be simple to operate. Again, drawing on the author's experience, where time recording systems fail this is normally due to the complexity of the documentation and the intricacies of the coding system.

In addition to a system for recording time spent on *quality cost activities,* there should also be a system which will allocate consumables, where used, to the respective costing category. For example, there may be travel and accommodation expenses incurred in dealing with a customer complaint, in which case these should be charged to failure/rectification cost under the appropriate code. If such costs were incurred in our hypothetical case then they would be charged to 89024-C3. The same would apply to communication expenses such as telephone, telex and facsimile.

There may be some classes of costs which could be extremely difficult, if not impossible, to isolate and allocate to the user's department or function such as new equipment or special test instruments. Such expenditure should be regarded as a capital cost and amortized over several years.

Develop a suitable accounting system
The development of a suitable accounting system could well be the most difficult part of the entire quality cost exercise. It will, inevitably, place an added responsibility on the accounting department and will, of necessity, require their utmost co-operation. The addition of quality cost codes, over and above the standard cost codes, almost certainly makes computerization of the accounting system imperative. Such a system should facilitate imme-

diate retrieval of information for analysis purposes. By setting up a quality cost register, it should be possible to produce a system to extract the relevant information from the data base and, by developing the appropriate software, assemble the data in the form required.

ANALYSIS OF THE QUALITY COSTS

Financial control of any business requires the appropriate methods of allocation and analysis of costs. The same applies to the control of quality. However, quality costing information is not produced to satisfy financial auditors and conflicts may arise between the requirements of auditors for corporate financial information and the requirements of management for quality cost information.

From the point of view of quality management, what will be demanded of the accounts department is a consistency of assessment rather than strict accuracy, so that trends can be discerned. Loss of reputation and therefore of future business cannot be assessed accurately but it is vital to have general agreement that the allocation of costs, although arbitrary, is fair and reasonable. Such cost could be referred to the working party finally to approve (see Chapter 4). Unfortunately, very few accountants are good at this sort of exercise — it goes against their training. It may be necessary, therefore, for the accounts staff, or a section of it, to be exposed to quality management education.

While on the subject of quality cost assessment, it is worthwhile mentioning that surveys carried out by a number of research organizations have revealed that for every customer who complains, nine will not complain but simply take their future business elsewhere. On the other side of the coin, however, a satisfied customer generally tells only four others. This represents a large imbalance between the recording of satisfaction versus dissatisfaction. These survey results could be used as a basis when allocating a cost to loss of reputation and subsequently the loss of future business, providing, of course, that customer complaints are documented and reviewed. This is particularly important in the service industry. The best advertisement is a satisfied customer. In many instances, unfortunately, customer complaints are 'hushed up' and management does not get to hear of them and is therefore not aware of their total implications.

Quality management will need financial information in order to balance the three quality cost elements of prevention, appraisal and failure/rectification. The most productive way of investing money is in prevention. Appraisal costs offer less return on investment as such costs do not prevent failure, they only identify failure. Nevertheless there will always be the need for some appraisal activity, if only to assure the quality of the item or service before its release to the customer and to minimize rejection after delivery. Failure/rectification costs are unplanned and must be considered as a loss of resource resulting in a reduction in profit.

It is vital, therefore, that all information pertaining to quality costs be readily and quickly available, in the right format and at all levels of management and supervision if it is to be used effectively.

COST OPTIMIZATION

The major purpose for developing a quality costing system is to optimize these costs effectively. An essential element of such optimization must be in the analysis of the quality cost data which must, in turn, rely on the accurate and prompt production of the costing information.

In the analysis of the data, due consideration should be given to the utilization of alternative methods. For example, in cases of sporadic failure, analysis of the situation might well reveal that rectification costs are insignificant compared with possible prevention costs. In such an instance, therefore, it is likely to be far more economic to rectify the deficiency as and when it should occur, rather than to develop and implement a system for prevention. Such a decision can be made only in light of all possible information.

An example of sporadic failure where prevention is less economic than rectification could be in the overbooking of seats in aeroplanes. This practice is a common one and used by airlines to guard against the no-show passenger and subsequent empty seats. On occasion some passengers cannot be found seats even though they have been booked in advance. This leads to all sorts of inducements, including long distance free flights, to persuade other passengers to give up their seats. This practice obviously pays the airlines or they would not do it. The airlines concerned will have evaluated the economics of prevention *vis-à-vis* failure/rectification and favoured the latter.

There are, of course, a number of caveats. One could not accept sporadic failures if safety is involved.

A finished product (item or service) does not normally come into existence as the result of a single activity; there are usually a number of intermediate processes involved before handover to the customer. The identification of a failure cost in any of these intermediates may result in additional appraisal measures being taken, with limited beneficial results. It is often found that the causes of high quality costs are not the result of the failure of a given process but the result of deficiencies elsewhere. The ultimate aim, in such instances, should be to discover those processes where preventative measures are weak, in other words to trace the problem back to its source and eliminate the cause.

REPORTING QUALITY COSTS

The purpose of any reporting system is to give the recipient information. Corrective action, where necessary, should be taken by the recipient and progress monitored. Action should be taken also to prevent a recurrence of the problem.

The responsibility for quality cost reporting is usually divided between the quality and accounting functions but the collection and processing of the

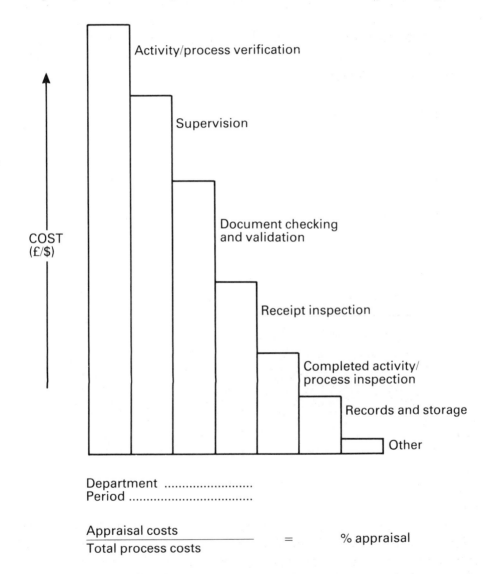

Fig. 3.1 — An example of a Pareto diagram indicating appraisal costs relative to a given period.

information is best left to the accounting function as this, being an independent service, usually enhances the credibility of the figures.

The publication of the figures is, again, best left to the accounting function but it should not be done in isolation. Other functions, particularly the quality function, should be actively involved in the planning of the format of the reports and the selection of the quality cost categories.

The format for presenting the quality cost information should be agreed. The reports should be easy to read and should be designed to communicate the pertinent information to the appropriate people. Reporting formats can be many and varied and can take the form of tabular structures, graphic information, barcharts, and Pareto diagrams. Examples of these various formats are given in Figs 3.1 and 3.2 and Table 3.1.

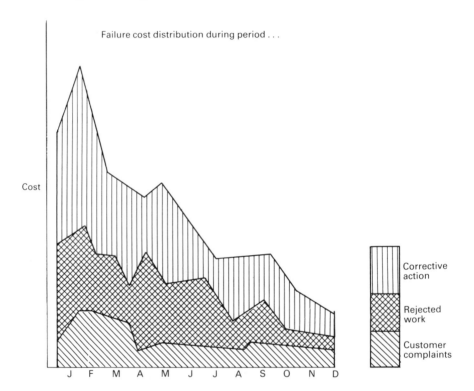

Fig. 3.2 — Typical failure cost analysis.

The information contained in these reports can be utilized to promote quality awareness throughout the entire organization. With the aid of attractively designed and presented graphic information the quality costs results could become discussion points at all personnel levels. Such infor-

Table 3.1 — Quality costs table by hours

QUALITY COSTS FOR PERIOD . . . .
Detailed analysis in hours by department

Code	Department				
	1	2	3	4	5
A1	6.5	6.5	4.1	8.6	2.4
A2	13.3	4.9	2.8	16.4	8.2
A3	4.0	2.0	3.5	4.5	2.0
A4	5.0	—	2.0	2.0	—
A	28.8	13.4	12.4	31.5	12.6
B1	8.0	6.5	5.5	8.5	3.8
B2	5.0	—	—	2.0	—
B3	1.0	1.5	2.0	3.0	2.5
B4	—	1.0	—	—	—
B	14.0	9.0	7.5	13.5	6.3
C1	—	—	—	—	—
C2	0.5	1.0	1.7	—	1.8
C3	—	2.0	—	3.4	—
C4	—	—	—	—	—
C	0.5	3.0	1.7	3.4	1.8
Summary					
A	28.8	13.4	12.4	31.5	12.6
B	14.0	9.0	7.5	13.5	6.3
C	0.5	3.0	1.7	3.4	1.8
	43.3	25.4	21.6	48.4	20.7

mation could show time lost owing to the occurrence of failure and improvements in the reduction of failure costs.

There is also the opportunity to promote awareness by all personnel towards reductions in quality costs. A number of organizations have adopted the concept of the *100-day club* which encourages employees to strive for error-free work for 100 days. At the end of that time, should the employee succeed, then the name of that employee is entered on the 100-day club register. One can then progress towards the 125-day club and so on. The concept of striving for 100 days of error-free work is not as easy as one would imagine. One hundred days constitutes 20 working weeks, which is approaching six months. In any event a responsible competitive attitude is fostered which can do only good for the company and its workforce. A similar concept is utilized very effectively in the safety field — the time during which there is no reportable accident.

Ultimately, quality cost data, if recorded accurately and categorized constructively into its various elements, will provide management with the information needed to make impartial and intelligent decisions on where, and in what strength, to attack the problem areas to meet corporate requirements. An analysis of the data will permit management to concentrate on those areas where control of such costs can have the greatest effect on the profitability of the organization. By forecasting the effects of changes in any one area, logical decisions can be taken to deploy personnel to the best advantage in order to make the most practical investment and thus enhance the profitability of the company.

4

Developing a quality management system

Come, give us a taste of your quality.

William Shakespeare, *Hamlet.*

THE RESPONSIBILITY FOR QUALITY

In any organization the senior executive is responsible for two things: the efficiency of the company and the quality of the service or product which that company provides.

In the public service sector he/she will be ultimately responsible to the government of the day and, in turn, the taxpayer, for the efficient running of the organization and for the service it gives to the community at large.

In the commercial environment, the senior executive of the larger organization will be ultimately responsible to the shareholders, both for the efficient running of the company and its profitability.

In the smaller organization, where the senior executive may well be the owner of the company, he/she will have a responsibility to the employees, to his/her family and, in all probability, to the bank manager, for the viability of the company.

Most people, particularly heads of families, will hold life assurance to protect their next of kin against the untimely death of the bread-winner and it is very unusual for this not to be the case. Yet, in small companies particularly, it is not uncommon to find that there is no visible quality management system in place, a system which can be seen to be working, although a quality management system is to the company what a life assurance policy is to the bread-winner of the family.

The life assurance policy will, providing the payments are regularly made, protect the family against sudden bereavement and will assist the family to keep going. A quality management system can be considered in the same light. It will, if regularly monitored for effectiveness, enable the company to keep going without losing momentum in the event of any changes in management or workforce. No company can be shielded from change and no person is immortal. We can all be struck down at any time and this could be catastrophic when the chief executive of a small company is unable to carry out his/her duties. Will the company be able to carry on without that person? With an effective quality management system in place and with a well-defined organizational structure developed to cope in such situations, the company can continue to thrive.

In the author's experience, it is not unusual for the chief executive of a company, particularly one of less than fifty employees, to be continually 'fighting fires'. This executive's desk is normally covered in paper and, generally, there is no hope of clearing that mass of paper without working excessively long hours and foregoing vacations. In the final analysis, the executive is usually well set for a heart attack or divorce — perhaps both.

Both situations can have an immediate detrimental effect on the company's viability. On questioning the executive why some of the work cannot be delegated to others, the answer is usually 'I have no one who I can trust to do it properly'. Invariably — although it will not be readily admitted — this is because the company has no documented quality management system and no well-defined organizational structure which allows for the delegation of tasks. A well-developed system will indicate when and how any task is to be properly undertaken and by whom.

FIRST CONSIDERATIONS

Any service organization, large or small, whether privately owned or not, can remain viable only if it gives a service which the customer wants at a price which the customer is prepared to pay. There are, therefore, two things which must be considered before embarking upon the development of a quality management system. The first is the need to satisfy customer requirements by providing a service which meets customer expectations, within budget and on schedule. The second is the requirement to supply such services in the most consistent, efficient and cost effective manner. Both of these can be achieved by introducing an effective quality management system.

Any company which is considering the development of such a system can experience problems with regard to the degree of detail with which the principles and practices of quality management are adopted.

It can be very easy to pay lip service to the entire concept, misleading customers, employees, partners, and even oneself, into believing that the system is functional. In such instances, the system exists only on paper and, because no effort is made to evaluate its implementation and effectiveness, it bears little resemblance to actual practice.

On the other hand, a company can strive mindlessly to control every activity and develop a system which is totally uneconomic, bureaucratic and a massive paper generator.

One, therefore, has to plan, develop and implement an economical, workable system which suits the company's operations and it is to the determination of such that due consideration must be given. Consequently, once having made a commitment to go ahead, a company should consider very carefully the corporate and regulatory requirements applicable to the business and should establish also the objectives for implementing such a system, which, as has already been said, could be to improve overall business performance with subsequent enhancement of profitability and greater customer satisfaction.

QUALITY MANAGEMENT SYSTEM DEVELOPMENT

It takes a great deal of time, effort and ability to develop and implement a quality management system and the task should be given the appropriate status and support. Both executive commitment and the allocation of appropriate resources are essential if the task is to succeed. At the end of the day success will be achieved only with leadership and teamwork.

As a first step, therefore, it will be necessary to embark upon an education and awareness campaign involving all employees including all levels of management. Senior management workshops are considered essential in this respect. In addition to the professional or technical requirements of a position, quality responsibilities should also take prominence.

Once the education process is under way it will then be necessary to review the existence and effectiveness of the current system. This review may reveal the need for additional procedures or routines to cover existing functions or activities not previously documented or controlled. This aspect will be discussed later. It will be a requirement also to establish the manpower, financial and equipment resources appropriate to the activities or functions involved in the development and eventual implementation of the quality management system.

Experience has shown that there are a number of steps to be taken in the planning, development and implementation of an effective system. These are:

(1) Appoint a quality management representative.
(2) Achieve acceptance of the quality management system.
(3) Establish a working party.
(4) Agree policy and objectives.

(5) Create staff awareness.
(6) Define responsibilities and lines of communication.
(7) Verify and agree the activities to be controlled.
(8) Document the quality management system.
(9) Implement the quality management system.
(10) Internal quality audits.
(11) Quality improvement.
(12) Management review.

Let us take each in turn.

(1) APPOINT A QUALITY MANAGEMENT REPRESENTATIVE

In the case of a very small company, the senior executive would be the ideal person to co-ordinate the development and implementation of the quality management system. Small companies may well be advised to appoint a consultant to assist in developing an effective system. Although what follows is mainly concerned with the larger organization the same principles apply to small organizations. As has been said, the difference is simply one of scale and application. In the larger organization it is not possible for the senior executive to co-ordinate the activity. It will be necessary, therefore, to appoint, in an executive position, a person who is to be responsible for this co-ordination. This person is usually known as the quality management representative or, in some cases, quality representative or even quality manager. The person so appointed must be given the responsibility and authority to co-ordinate all activities, oversee the development of the documented system and monitor and verify the eventual implementation and effectiveness of the system.

This would mean that, in essence, the person so appointed would be given the responsibility and authority to represent the company on all matters pertinent to the quality management system and would be independent of other functions. This person would need to report directly to the chief executive.

The primary responsibilities of a quality management representative would be to:

— co-ordinate the structure of the quality management system, which should involve all departments of the company;
— determine the company's policy on quality;
— determine the company's quality objectives;
— review the organizational relationships as they affect quality;
— monitor the implementation and effectiveness of the system;
— determine and report the principal causes of quality losses and non-conformances;

— develop proposals for improvement.

These principles equally apply to small companies.

All companies employ someone to be responsible for the accuracy of its financial matters and, in the main, that person occupies an executive position. That person is usually aware of the costs associated with such matters as absenteeism, holidays and downtime, and the senior executive will be required to present a complete financial statement to the authorities and, where necessary, to the company shareholders. It is only rarely that a company will employ an executive who is responsible for quality yet, as we have seen, a company's quality costs (the cost of inveterate waste) can be equal to or, in many cases, even exceed the profit margin of that company.

It is necessary, therefore, that the person appointed as the quality management representative has the appropriate responsibility and authority. Executive status for this position would be considered an advantage. It is necessary, therefore, for this person to have management capabilities. The ability to communicate at all levels would be an essential requirement. Knowledge and experience of the service industry sector are also essential requirements, as are the understanding and application of quality management systems. This is an important position and great care should be taken in the appointment of such a person.

This person, once appointed, would, as has been already stated, represent the senior executive and would determine, with other management, the functions to be controlled.

(2)   ACHIEVE ACCEPTANCE OF THE QUALITY MANAGEMENT SYSTEM

As has already been said, an effective quality management system will involve all departments and functions. Such a system can be developed only with the full participation and co-operation of all concerned, who must be given the opportunity in helping to develop the system. A system that has been thoroughly discussed and agreed is much more likely to achieve the desired objectives than one which is imposed — whoever does the imposing!

Management's role
The senior management of an organization has a very important part to play in this respect. All must have a very clear grasp of the concepts of quality management and must be enthused by it and be able to apply its principles and practices to their own departments and functions. Management must also have the ability to motivate their subordinates and to ensure their continued commitment to the cause.

Invariably the introduction of the system will lead to change and most people are against change, even if it is manifestly for the better. Experience has shown that, in the early stages of implementation, the most common reason for the failure of the project has been due to the obstructive attitudes of managers who resent change; although they may appear outwardly to be keen and committed, they are inwardly apprehensive and insecure. Such attitudes are generally the result of insufficient information and support from their superiors. One is quite likely to come across such entrenched attitudes as:

— 'Why change now; we have always done it this way?'
— 'Our general level of quality is good enough as it is.'
— 'Fire-fighting is exciting and makes the job worthwhile.'

Only by education, awareness and involvement can such attitudes be altered.

There is, therefore, the need for managers to work more closely with their subordinates and a review of the 12 C's as detailed in Chapter 1 may well be appropriate at this time.

It is worthwhile expending a great deal of time and effort in obtaining this co-operation and acceptance. It is necessary, therefore, for the respective department and/or function heads to be involved in determining the activities which will have an impact on quality as determined by efficiency, profitability and customer acceptance.

With the best will in the world, quality management will not succeed of its own accord. It takes time, effort and considerable planning and it will be necessary, therefore, to develop a strategy for its implementation. A policy stating the objectives of the project and signifying the commitment of the chief executive must be also developed.

Of necessity, the strategy development and policy making must take place at the very highest level of the organization. This can be achieved, in the first instance, by forming a working party, which should comprise representatives from all the departments and/or functions concerned.

(3) ESTABLISH A WORKING PARTY

The responsibility for the formation of the working party should lie with the person who has been appointed to the representative position.

The working party should be chaired by the senior executive of the organization, with the quality management representative acting as co-ordinator. This working party should include representatives from all the departments and/or functions concerned and these representatives should be, preferably, the heads of departments and/or functions. Where this is not possible, then the representative should be given power of attorney to act for the respective head. The members of the working party should be determined by executive management. The working party, once established, should remain a permanent feature of the company with clear terms of reference, including the approval of arbitrary cost allocations as discussed in Chapter 3.

This working party should be responsible subsequently for reviewing, on a regular basis, the effectiveness of the entire system and for the initiation of improvements.

(4) AGREE POLICY AND OBJECTIVES

Initially the working party's responsibility will be to agree the policy and objectives for developing the system and to establish the framework appropriate to the company and the services it offers.

Generally, a company's objectives in implementing a quality management system are twofold:

(1) satisfying customer expectations;
(2) improvement in overall business efficiency.

The first can be achieved by the utilization of an appropriate national quality system standard as a guide. In the main, at first sight, the majority of standards of this sort would appear to be inapplicable to most service industries but, as will be seen later, this is certainly not the case.

The second will be brought about as the result of the first, provided one treats the application of quality management as a company-wide activity. All departments and functions should be included — administration (office management and secretarial), commercial, market research, after-sales service, and public relations — and not just those related to the services given. Shortcomings in any of these areas could lead to a reduction in efficiency and profitability which could, in turn, impact upon the business as a whole.

The objectives discussed above are the two key issues which form the basis for development and implementation. There are many other objectives which could be considered, such as:

— the reduction of inveterate waste,
— increasing customer confidence,
— increasing employee participation and morale,
— to become a market leader in the area,
— to maintain a competitive position in the market-place,
— to comply with customer quality system requirements,
— to obtain second or third party registration.

Once the objectives have been decided upon, such objectives could form the basis of the company's documented policy for quality. (The policy statement is discussed in detail in Chapter 6).

(5) CREATE STAFF AWARENESS

Management should then ensure that this policy is understood and accepted at all levels of the organization. Without this agreement and acceptance, the implementation of the system will be difficult to achieve.

These awareness sessions should put forward the reasons why the company is embarking upon such a project and the resultant expected benefits. Wherever possible, it is recommended that such sessions should be carried out by third-party sources — a consultant. In the author's experience, by utilizing the capabilities of someone outside the organization much greater credence is given to the subject. The utilization of third-party sources has been found to lead to a much greater employee acceptance (a prophet from another country, so to speak). The skilled consultant, by listening and discussion, will carry the staff along with him/her so well that the quality system becomes *their* system. Once this is achieved, success is almost guaranteed.

Again, experience has shown that co-operation is more easily obtained if these 'awareness' sessions are conducted at the very earliest possible moment. In this way all employees can prepare and possibly highlight problem areas which exist because of inadequate controls. By this means, personnel can be made to appreciate that they will be part of the system and that it will work to their benefit only if they co-operate. Systems have been known to have limited success, or even result in failure, owing to inadequate staff awareness of the reasons for, and the benefits of, a well-prepared and implemented quality management system.

The style and method of communication can have a profound effect upon the acceptance of the system. Attitudes of the employees are very important and will reflect the degree to which they understand and support management policies.

Inherent in these awareness sessions must be an effective feedback mechanism, which will channel information back to the working party. This feedback mechanism must be available at all times and will be particularly important once the system is up and running. It will allow for accurate monitoring of the effectiveness of the system and, where necessary, permit changes to be made.

(6) DEFINE RESPONSIBILITIES AND LINES OF COMMUNICATION

In many organizations a person's responsibilities are not clearly defined. There is a tendency to appoint someone to a given position and then to delegate additional responsibilities to that person as he or she becomes more proficient and experienced. As time goes on, this person reaches supervisory or management status purely by taking on these additional responsibilities and then, when things go wrong, it becomes exceedingly difficult to identify the cause or the source of the problem.

All responsibilities should be documented in the form of job descriptions, which should include as a minimum:
— the title or description of the position
— the grade or level of the position
— the reporting structure of the position
— whether or not the position carries any supervisory responsibilities
— the primary responsibilities of that position
— the knowledge and experience required to fill that position
— and the quality responsibility of the position.

The activity of developing job descriptions will involve liaising with all employees and when the individuals are questioned on what they believe to be their responsibilities there will inevitably be duplications and overlaps. There could well be instances of activities not being completely covered as the demarcation lines had not been sufficiently clear and explicit. This in itself is, in the author's experience, the cause of many so-called quality problems.

The exposure and elimination of the duplication of activities is a sensitive area and must be done with care and consideration, otherwise it could well lead to ill-feeling and resentment among employees who may feel that their jobs are in jeopardy. This must not happen!

In addition to documenting job descriptions, it is advisable to formulate a promotion or career progression chart, which will tie in with the relevant grade or level of any given position. This information should be available to all employees and it will help in giving them a sense of belonging, which will inevitably lead to a greater responsibility to the company and ultimately achieving the efficiency required to produce the services and/or items fit for purpose and right first time, every time.

Once the job descriptions have been documented then, with the information which has been obtained, it will be possible to formulate organization charts for each of the departments concerned. These charts will enable each grade, or level of employee, to understand and accept where their position is located within the hierarchy and to whom each person reports.

Organization charts can be established for individual departments and/or disciplines but they will not achieve integration if they are developed in isolation. No department can work in isolation. There is always the need to liaise with others. For example, sales must liaise with the service department, administration and finance. An organization chart which identifies these interfaces should, therefore, be developed. Where interfaces are established, then of course these would be documented in the appropriate job description and work procedure. This detailed organization chart will ultimately identify the primary positions and reporting routes of the company.

In some companies known to the author, the company chairman has insisted on the head of the organization being at the bottom of the chart, with those having direct contact with the customer at the top, thus indicating that the chief executive supports the whole organization.

(7)   VERIFY AND AGREE THE ACTIVITIES TO BE CONTROLLED

This activity will eventually determine the effectiveness of the system and an in-depth consideration of what needs to be controlled is essential. The quality system standards can give useful guidance in this instance. There are many national standards in prominence but that which is gaining the greatest acceptance is the International Standard (ISO) 9000 series.

This series of standards relates, in the main, to design/development, production, installation and servicing of a product but can act as a useful guide to any company embarking upon the development and implementation of a quality management system (see Table 4.1).

It will be noted that there are 20 requirements associated with the ISO

Table 4.1 — Quality System Requirements ISO 9001–1987

1. Management responsibility
2. Quality system
3. Contract review
4. Design control
5. Document control
6. Purchasing
7. Purchaser supplied product
8. Product identification and traceability
9. Process control
10. Inspection and testing
11. Inspection, measuring and test equipment
12. Inspection and test status
13. Control of non-conforming product
14. Corrective action
15. Handling, storage, packaging and delivery
16. Quality records
17. Internal quality audits
18. Training
19. Servicing
20. Statistical techniques

9000 series and, at first glance, it would appear that the majority relate only to manufacturing. This, however, is not the case. If the list of requirements is examined closely it will be seen that at least ten of them are applicable to any organization, large or small, regardless of its product. They are:

— management responsibility (organization),
— the quality system (work instructions),
— contract review (planning),
— documentation control,
— purchasing,
— control of non-conforming product,
— corrective action,
— records,
— internal quality audits,
— training.

These are the author's 'ten essential elements of a quality management system' and are the subject of Chapter 5.

However, over and above these 'ten essentials', thought has then to be given to the other business functions which require control and, in so doing, the risk, cost and benefit considerations must be evaluated, both for the company and for the customer.

In the case of the company, consideration must be given to the risks involved in relation to the production of a deficient item or service where such a deficiency could lead to high-cost rectification work, liability claims, loss of market share, customer complaints and others.

In the case of the customer, consideration must be given to the risks involved in relation to the health and safety of people, dissatisfaction with the product (goods and services), availability, claims under guarantees, loss of confidence and others.

It is therefore imperative that due consideration is given in determining which functions, if not properly controlled, are likely to have a detrimental effect on the business.

A quality management system must, therefore, be beneficial both to the company and to the customer.

ISO 9000 states:

An effective quality management system should be designed to satisfy customer needs and expectations while serving to protect the company's interests. A well-structured quality system is a valuable management resource in the optimization and control of quality in relation to risk, cost and benefit considerations.

In determining the functions to be controlled, one must realize that the system developed must be economical and effective. Experience again has shown that other reasons why a quality management system fails to achieve the desired results are usually due to:

— insufficient focus on the company's business objectives;
— an increase in bureaucracy, resulting in management time being taken up discussing concepts, thus leading to increased paperwork rather than action;
— the generation of a large number of projects which have no priority or direction.

Consequently, it is not wholly surprising that the results are occasionally poor. The word *quality* has, in many instances, left the responsibility for quality management with the quality department rather than with management itself and quite often this department has been under-resourced and deprived of the skills required to ensure the success of the initiative.

These negative aspects do not, however, invalidate the basic tenets of quality management. In fact they confirm, quite simply, that it is not a panacea for all ills and they also indicate where improvements can be made.

It cannot be over-emphasized that management commitment and support is essential if the project is to be successful. This commitment needs to be at the highest level, with the emphasis on leadership if the momentum is to be maintained. A successful management system has no finite end, it is a continuous process of improvement and thus requires adequate resources to ensure its success.

In the final analysis, however, the purpose of quality management is to improve the overall performance, profitability and efficiency of the business in what is becoming an increasingly competitive market-place.

The criteria for the control of an activity or function must, therefore, lie in the aspects of default. What one must consider is the result of a deficiency in relation to the risk and the cost involved, not only in rectification but in the cost of implementing a system to control the activity itself. The more controls one implements the greater the cost — but to what effect?

Consider this analogy. In the era of the hour-glass figure, Edwardian ladies were wont to make use of an undergarment known as a corset. The tighter this garment was drawn the more waspish the figure but the detrimental effects were to limit the capacity of the lungs and in, times of stress or heat, the poor suffering female was apt to faint (Fig. 4.1). The same could be said of an over-controlled management system. The more systems imposed, the more bureaucratic it becomes and the economics of the system are defeated. Consider, therefore, the word CORSET and when identifying whether or not an activity, over and above the ten essentials, should be controlled ask oneself in the event that the activity should go wrong:

Fig. 4.1.

What is the **CO**st of putting it right?
What are the **R**esources required to put it right?
What are the **S**afety implications should it go wrong?
What are the **E**nvironmental impacts should it go wrong?
What is the **T**ime involved in putting it right?

If the answer to one or more of these questions is 'substantial' then one should implement a system to control that activity. If, on the other hand, the answer to all the questions is 'minimal' then it is possibly more economical to correct a deficiency whenever it occurs rather than spend time, effort and money in developing a documented system to control the activity in the off chance that it should be defective. If one considers the 'ten essential elements' in this light it will be apparent that a deficiency occurring in any of them could have a substantial impact throughout the entire organization and result in considerable detrimental implications relating to any of the 'corset' considerations.

The determination of the activities to be controlled and the methods by which they are to be controlled is the most important step in the development of a quality system and must be treated with great care.

(8)   DOCUMENT THE QUALITY MANAGEMENT SYSTEM

When all the major activities have been identified, then a brief outline describing what is done to control these activities can be documented. These outlines will assist in determining the procedural requirements and they can also be utilized in the formulation of a quality manual should such a document be required.

It should be noted that an effective quality management system actually *reduces* paperwork. This is because its generation and control are properly structured.

The requirements for, and the development of a quality manual, are dealt with in Chapter 6.

A typical outline for the control of documentation is given in Appendix A, outline 2. It will be noted from this outline that there are a number of subsidiary activities involved in controlling documentation. These subsidiary activities should be covered by means of individual procedures. We have mentioned the manual and procedures and it will be seen that a number of 'levels' or 'tiers' of documentation are being developed. These are:

The quality manual.
Procedures.
Job instructions.
Forms and records.

These 'tiers' of documentation are shown in Fig. 4.2, which will be explained fully later in Chapter 6.

Having documented the system outlines, the next step is to develop the procedure index.

As has been shown, each system outline will result in a number of activities which are to be procedurally controlled. These activities should now be listed and indexed. All procedures should carry a document number as the procedures themselves will eventually form part of the company's document or library system. A numbering system should be developed which will identify the procedure to the department or function which implements it. Such procedures should not be annotated as quality management documents as this could result in an implication that the quality department is responsible for them. A typical numbering system could be as follows:

XYZ-DOC-001

where XYZ represents the company's identity, DOC represents the document control department function and 001 represents the document number.

The title of the document would also be indicated, for example:

XYZ-DOC-001 Numbering System for XYZ Company Limited documents.

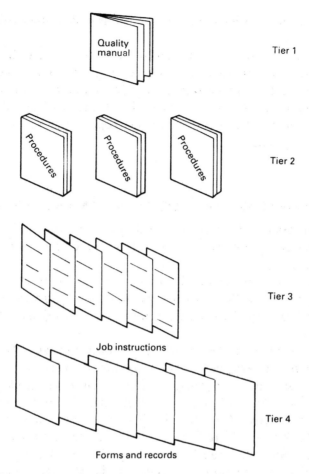

Fig. 4.2 — The four tiers of documentation.

Procedures which are to be implemented by more than one department are normally of an administrative nature and could, therefore, be identified as:

XYZ-ADM-001

and so on.

Once an index has been developed, it should be kept updated. If it is found that a particular procedure is no longer relevant and can be discontinued, then the number allocated to that procedure should be declared obsolete and not used again, the procedure index being annotated accordingly.

Once the system element outlines and the procedures index have been produced, then it will be possible to identify responsibilities for the authorship of procedures. Full details of procedural development are given in Chapter 6.

The procedure index can be utilized also to identify those procedures which already exist and those which have to be written to complete the total system. The exercise of reviewing existing documentation may well highlight the existence of duplicate or similar documents and possibly documents which are obsolete. This presents a good opportunity for reappraisal and a 'spring cleaning' session.

(9)   IMPLEMENT THE QUALITY MANAGEMENT SYSTEM

This implementation stage will involve the co-operation of all concerned and, to obtain this co-operation, all employees must understand the reasons for implementation.

The first requirement should be for the chief executive to launch the initiative by means of the policy statement discussed earlier, ensuring that its message and its requirements are understood throughout all levels of the organization.

Communicate to all employees the reasons for, and the benefits to be obtained from, the implementation of a quality management system.

This is best done by holding a series of awareness talks, or seminars, starting with senior management, through all levels to junior personnel. No one should be left out. Co-operation is usually more easily obtained before any procedural controls are documented but after the policy statement has been written and approved. In this way all employees can prepare and possibly highlight problem areas which exist because of inadequate controls. By this means, personnel can be made to appreciate that they are a part of the system and that it will work to their benefit only if they co-operate.

For this to succeed, training is essential at all levels to ensure that everyone in the workforce has the knowledge and 'tools' appropriate to their place in the organization and the role they have to play in the quality management system.

The requirement for review should also be emphasized and this should include information on the necessity for both system and compliance audits. The word 'audit' may well tend to frighten some staff as they may expect to be supervised continuously and suspect that management is adopting the 'big brother' attitude. It should be made clear to them that audits, as will be explained later, are carried out first to assess the adequacy of the system and only secondarily to verify compliance with instructions. Audits involve two-way communication.

It should be emphasized that each individual is responsible for the quality of the work produced and that reliance for quality cannot be placed on others subsequently to confirm that the required quality standard has been reached. 'Right first time, every time' should be everyone's intent. This is the prime goal of any quality system.

(10) INTERNAL QUALITY AUDITS

As has been explained, once the quality management system is implemented it will be necessary to monitor it continuously to verify firstly that the system is effective and secondly that the system is being complied with. The internal quality audit will identify any shortcomings which may indicate trends towards particular non-conformances and can also indicate areas where quality improvement is possible.

The subject of audits is dealt with in Chapter 7.

(11) QUALITY IMPROVEMENT

Once the system is found to be effective and the initial objectives have been achieved then effort can be expended in improvement. There are a number of techniques associated with quality improvement and these are dealt with in Chapter 8. Once improvements are made, these are integrated into the system and subject also to audit. It will be seen, therefore, that quality improvement is a continuous exercise and there is no finite end to the implementation of a quality management system. It is imperative that the senior executive, together with senior management, are continually involved with the entire process and it will, therefore, be necessary for them to undertake a regular review of the total system.

(12) MANAGEMENT REVIEW

The review of the management system is again a separate subject and is dealt with in Chapter 9.

5

The ten essential elements of a quality management system

The elements be kind to thee, and make thy spirits all of comfort.
W. Shakespeare, *Antony and Cleopatra*.

The essential elements of a quality management system which were considered to be applicable to any organization, large or small, regardless of product (item or service), were touched upon briefly in Chapter 4. and it was determined that there are ten of them and, to recap, they are:

(1) management responsibility (organization),
(2) the quality system (work instructions),
(3) contract review (planning),
(4) document control,
(5) purchasing,
(6) control of non-conforming product,
(7) corrective action,
(8) records,
(9) internal quality audits,
(10) training.

It is now worthwhile examining these elements in detail.

(1) MANAGEMENT RESPONSIBILITY (ORGANIZATION)

As for any organization, whether service or manufacturing related, the responsibility for, and commitment to, quality belongs to the highest level of management. It is therefore most important for management to define, develop and document its policy relating to the type of service to be provided and the methods to be used in achieving service quality objectives. This was discussed earlier.

There is also the necessity under this heading to define the company's organizational structure and to identify the responsibility authority and the interrelation of all personnel who manage, perform and verify quality.

This is a very wide sweeping statement and if interpreted in its fullest sense will include all employees. This means, quite rightly, that all employees are, and should be, responsible for the quality of the work they produce and should not rely on others subsequently to check the results. The first check in the quality management chain is the 'self-check'. However, where there is a requirement for an independent check on a service activity then this should be specifically defined.

(2)   THE QUALITY SYSTEM (WORK INSTRUCTIONS)

A documented system is the *sine qua non* of effective quality management; without it there would be no means of knowing what has to be done, how and by whom. Additionally, without a documented system there would be no means to establish and verify whether the system is effective. The types of documentation have already been introduced in the previous chapter and are dealt with in detail in later chapters of this book.

(3)   CONTRACT REVIEW (PLANNING)

A service organization commits itself to providing a service of some kind and a business is developed on that basis. The details of the service requirements can be determined by two means. Firstly by the customer specifically detailing the requirements (the specified needs) or secondly by market research and analysis. The results of the market research and its subsequent analysis, or the detailed specified requirements, could be construed as a contract and it is therefore important that all details of the service require-ments are reviewed by all concerned.

Every company should review its contract to determine that the require-ments are understood. A method of reviewing customer requirements and planning for the contract execution is most important and should be carried out regardless of the size or nature of the service contract. Even the small company, when receiving an order from a customer, normally carries out a contract review activity without perhaps recognizing it as such, by reading the order and then determining what actions, materials, personnel and perhaps equipment are required to deal adequately and efficiently wty the cus-tomer's requirements. In many instances, however, this activity is not documented but it occurs just the same. Perhaps it would be beneficial if it were to be documented even by the simple utilization of a check-list to ensure that nothing has been forgotten.

There should be no stigma attached to the use of check-lists; they are an *aide memoire* and serve to remind us what should be considered. Check-lists are particularly valuable when time is short as it is usually in situations of panic when things are forgotten.

In the case of the larger organization where numbers of staff are involved, the contract review activity should be documented in order that the necessary co-ordination, liaison and understanding of customer requirements can be achieved and can be seen to have been achieved.

Contract review is an activity which probably highlights the greatest differences in planning for a service as compared with a manufactured item. Often, however, there is a very large element of subjective judgement attached to service quality and direct measurement or quantification of the service to be provided is very difficult to determine but it should obviously be done where possible. For example, in a bar or pub, the quantity of one's pint (or litre) of bitter can be (and should be) accurately measured, as can its specific gravity and alcohol content for that matter. What cannot be measured is its taste — or the quality of the sandwiches which one may buy at the same time. However, the beer is likely to taste all right if it has been properly stored and looked after. Similarly, the sandwiches will be more likely to be of acceptable quality if the bread and contents are fresh.

The execution of a service, however, should include this activity and such should be undertaken before any work commences. All concerned should be aware of their responsibilities and an appropriate team assembled to review the contract and to plan its execution. The 'team' could comprise a number of people or even a single person. In any event, due consideration should be given to a number of issues, which would include:

(a) work scope,
(b) customer requirements (stated or implied),
(c) staffing levels and experience,
(d) material requirements,
(e) organization.

(a) Work scope
The review should entail a detailed consideration of the scope of work to verify that the requirements are adequately defined and understood. Should a service contract have been subject to tender then this review would also identify any conditions which may differ from those in the tender. Any such differences should be resolved with the customer immediately.

(b) Customer requirements (stated or implied)
Are there any special conditions which are out of the ordinary? If so, these should be evaluated to verify that the company has the capability to meet these requirements.

(c) Staffing levels and experience
Consideration should be given to the number of staff required to complete the service contract on time, together with the experience and qualifications of such staff. The methods for managing the service should be also established at this stage together with the designation of the appropriate service procedures and routines.

(d) Material requirements
It should be ensured that, where required, the correct materials and quantities are available. Such materials usually comprise tools of the trade and could range from stationery through cleaning materials, drugs, etc., depending on the nature of the business. Where materials have to be ordered, then the sources of such materials should be assessed, together with delivery, price and quality. The actual mechanics of this activity will be covered under purchasing.

(e) Organization
Who does what in the task force assigned to the contract? Who reports to whom and what are each individual's terms of reference? If the organization is well-defined and made generally known immediately, then there can be no misconceptions about reporting responsibilities. A considerable amount of time and misunderstanding can be avoided when the right person to approach concerning any given issue is known. Of course, the same philosophies must apply in the corporate sense. Many companies do not set up contact organizations as such but the organizational structure should still exist.

(4) DOCUMENT CONTROL

Every company produces documents of some sort or another and their control is most important. There is no department which does not come under the umbrella of document control. In the author's experience, this is the most neglected of activities and many of the problems which arise are due to inadequate control in this area.

Documents in this context cover letters, invoices, legal briefs, specifications, procedures, data sheets, purchase orders, minutes of meetings, and so on. These should be presented in a correct and uniform manner. Personnel quite often have different ideas on how documents should be formulated. Minutes of meetings are a case in point. Experience has shown that in many companies there is no corporate policy for the format of minutes. Departments are given no guidance in this respect and minutes are produced in a manner considered appropriate by the person concerned. This lack of uniformity makes the eventual auditing of the system very difficult. It is important, therefore, that minutes of meetings should always state:

— reason for convening the meeting,
— agenda,
— those attending,
— duration,
— decisions reached,
— action to be taken and by whom,
— follow-up procedure.

A uniform approach should be agreed, defined and communicated to all concerned. Uniform documentation presentation helps to avoid errors and facilitates checking, allowing more use of standard checking routines. It is far easier to handle documents when, for example, the document number, contract number, or such other identifier, can always be found in the same place, or when the contents lists of similar documents are in the same order. It is difficult and time-consuming to check documents whose contents are distributed in different patterns or sequences.

Document identification should be standardized and controlled using logical procedures. Complex numbering systems should be avoided, as these tend to confuse rather than assist in identification and retrieval of documents. The simpler the system, the easier it is to operate and control.

It is recommended that identification systems should, as a minimum, contain the following information:

— service or customer identification,
— document type (denoting whether it is an instruction, purchase requisition, routine, brief, etc.),
— the serial number of the document,
— the date,
— the document revision status.

The following is a typical arrangement for document identification:

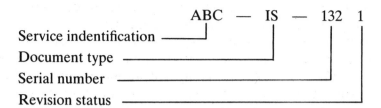

Document approval procedures should be formalized and those who carry the authority to approve documents should be named. Specimen sets of signatures and initials should be registered in the appropriate records.

Document checking, including amendments

Where document checking is essential, then checking routines should be formulated. These routines should include, as a minimum, the types of documents to be checked, the methods of checking and the personnel responsible for the check. It is important to establish the types of documents to be checked. This is a management decision.

The same principle applies to the approval of documents. Those which require approval and by whom the approval is to be given should be clearly stated. It is as well to specify those which do not require such approval so as to avoid misunderstanding.

Document amendments

The checking and approval of amendments to documents should be similarly formalized, together with a system for the retrieval and disposal of superseded documents.

It has been found that many companies experience great difficulties in withdrawing superseded documents from point of use. There are a number of ways in which this can be satisfactorily achieved.

The first is physically to exchange the superseded document. A very effective method in the small company within one location but very time-consuming in the large multi-departmental or multi-divisional organization.

The second is to rely on the recipient of the amended copy to destroy the superseded document. This method has been found not to be totally effective. However, experience has shown that where the recipient is responsible for destroying the superseded document, then it is better to instruct them to acknowledge that they have done so. A system employed by the author is to enclose the amended document with a duplicated covering transmittal note which is in two distinct parts.

The first part of the transmittal contains an acknowledgement of the amended document, for which a signature is required. The second part contains a confirmation that the superseded document has been destroyed. Fig. 5.1 is a typical example of such a transmittal note.

This method has been found to be quite effective. There are cases, of course, where the recipient has not destroyed the superseded document but they are rare. The physical act of signing that one has destroyed a document makes one think twice before appending a signature. Furthermore, subsequent audits of the document control system will highlight any shortcomings.

Document distribution

In large companies, and in these days of readily available (if expensive) photocopying, the sending of copies of all documents to everyone who might conceivably be interested in seeing them is all too common. Such instances are counter-productive and self-defeating. Procedures should, therefore, be established to identify which documents are really needed by selected recipients. Many people may wish to be included on the distribution list whether they need to be or not. Involvement by those who have no need to get involved creates confusion. A matrix chart which lists document types along the left-hand vertical column and has the remaining columns headed with all potential recipients, is a useful and concise method for denoting the standard distribution arrangements for documents. In the matrix, each box will link a document type with a possible addressee and the matrix will automatically cover all possible permutations. It is simply necessary to leave blank boxes where there is to be no distribution. In each case where documents need to be sent to an addressee, the number of sets to be sent is written in the relevant box. It is stressed again that this should be arranged strictly on a 'need to know' rather than a 'want to know' basis.

A formalized procedure for distribution is also essential to ensure not only that each person who requires documents appears on the list so that he or she gets them in the first place, but also to ensure that they are in the right quantities, of the correct form and of the latest revision.

With the advent of the desk top computer, document control has become much simpler with regard to documents for internal use. A central data input can amend documents immediately and the information readily accessed by those who need to know. However, it will still be necessary to retain hard copies of documents to retain an audit trail in the case of previous amendments. Authorization is also difficult to identify from a 'monitor' and, therefore, the hard copy of the authorized document should be retained for record and audit purposes.

Retention, retrieval, storage and handover

The procedures to be implemented to control document retention, retrieval, storage and handover should be established. In all probability there will be specific legislative or contractual requirements for the retention of docu-

```
                    DOCUMENT TRANSMITTAL No.....


To............:     Department..........        Date..........

From..........     Department..........        Date.........

Document No:....... Document Title..............Rev.No........

i)  This document is a first issue.                    (*)
ii) This document supersedes Rev.No......Copy No(s)........(*)
(* delete as appropriate)




Enclosed is/are controlled copy number(s)...... of the above
referenced document for your information and retention.

As required by procedure No.DOC.008, please complete section A
and, where appropriate (see ii above), section B of both the
original and duplicate of this transmittal notice. The duplicate
shall be returned to the originator within 5 days of receipt and
the original retained on file for audit purposes.



Originator...............(signed)

--------------------------------------------/------------------
Section A


I confirm receipt of copy number(s)..... of the captioned
document(s)



Signed....................        Date...........

-------------------------------------------------------------

Section B (see ii above)

I confirm having destroyed my controlled copy No(s)...... of the
superseded document.



Signed....................        Date...........

-------------------------------------------------------------

Form Doc.0083
```

Fig. 5.1.

ments and records generated during the execution of the service or contract. For example, many sector-based quality assurance schemes demand a limited period for retention of documents. The safety-related industries may be required to retain documents for 25 years or more; hospital patient records and legal records are other cases in point. Provision should be made to fulfil these requirements.

The longer the retention period the more susceptible the documents will become to damage and/or loss; therefore provision should be made for proper storage and for the method of storage to be adopted. If hard copies are to be retained, then space becomes a major factor, as does the size and type of the containers to be used. The storage problem can be minimized by the use, if approved, of microfilm.

Whatever the retention period and storage methods, there should be a system installed to facilitate ease of retrieval should the need arise — as is very often the case.

On contract completion, if there is a requirement that documents must be handed over to the customer, then a method of handover should be documented.

All these requirements should be considered during the planning stage of an activity and not left until documents start to be generated.

Regardless of company size, there is always the need properly to control documentation.

(5)   PURCHASING

All companies large or small, regardless of the service they offer, purchase items or the services of people and in many instances such purchased items or services may be critical to the safety and efficiency of the service supplied by the prime organization. It is, therefore, important that the purchasing activity is given the same attention with regard to planning and control as all other activities. It is important also that the purchasing organization should establish a good working relationship with its suppliers and therefore essential that purchasing activities be evaluated and controlled. Even in the very small company one should undertake an evaluation of what is to be purchased and the initial stage of this evaluation may be no more than thumbing through the 'Yellow Pages' to identify possible suitable sources of supply.

Once having identified these possible sources of supply, one should then assess the supplier to verify that:

— the requirements can be met,
— the quality is acceptable,
— the delivery schedule is acceptable,

— the price is right.

All too often price is a major factor and an evaluation is made on that aspect alone. One gets what one pays for and 'the bitterness of poor quality remains long after the sweetness of low price is forgotten'.

A proper evaluation of procurement sources can eliminate major problems later on. This applies not only to the purchase of items but also to the purchase of services (people). Expanding on this assessment process, one can ensure that, to all intents and purposes, the purchased item or service will meet specified requirements by the adoption of a system that considers the following:

— the service or item to be supplied,
— the quality of that service or item,
— the cost of the service or item,
— delivery.

The type of bought-in services can be many and varied depending upon the nature of the business in which one is engaged. These bought-in services can include drafting, janitorial, nursing, security, and the like.

Materials can range from standard stationery items to very sophisticated pharmaceutical products.

The selection of suppliers, and the extent of control exercised by the purchaser, should therefore take into consideration the type of service/ product and, where appropriate, the records of the suppliers' previously demonstrated capability and performance.

The methods of selecting a supplier can take many forms. A history of a supplier's capability can be established purely on a quality/delivery/price record. Where a supplier makes frequent and regular deliveries to a customer, then confidence is maintained on a continuing basis. This method of selection should be documented and updated by delivery analyses.

Similarly, with the supply of 'people' to fulfil given tasks, a similar approach can be adopted.

In other instances, one could verify a supplier's capability either by inspecting the item(s) at the supplier's premises before delivery or by incoming inspection upon receipt. Although effective, this may not be very economical when an item is rejected. This method of selection should also be documented and updated by inspection results.

The responsibility for quality should be with the supplier and it should not be necessary for the customer to 'inspect' quality into supplied items although, unfortunately, it very often is. In the case of very complex purchased items or the requirement for the supply of very highly qualified personnel, then such methods of selection would not be very meaningful. It will be necessary, therefore, particularly if the supply source is unknown, to carry out an assessment to verify whether or not the potential supplier is capable of meeting not only the quality requirements but the product/service, delivery and economic requirements. Such an assessment would, therefore, fall into three distinct parts:

— an evaluation of the product/service
— quality
— cost and delivery.

Evaluation of the product/service
An evaluation should be made of the potential supplier to verify whether he has the capability to supply the item or the service required.

Quality
An evaluation should be made of the supplier's own quality management system. This would be documented and the evaluation would verify whether that quality system is being effectively implemented and receives full support of senior management.

At this stage, with no contract made, there is nothing binding upon a potential supplier to conform to any given requirement. It is possible only to review the quality system and to make observations on any apparent deficiency; perhaps advising the supplier that the deficiency; if not rectified, could have an adverse affect on contract award.

Cost and delivery
An evaluation should be made of the potential supplier's prices and delivery record. Have prices for similar contracts been competitive and is there a proven ability to deliver the item, or provide the service, on time?

As has been said, when finally settling upon a supplier (or suppliers), it is important to develop a good working relationship with the supplier(s) and to establish a good communication channel so that the mechanism exists for improving quality and for resolving quality disputes in an expeditious manner when the need arises.

(6)   CONTROL OF NON-CONFORMING PRODUCT

A *product* does not necessarily mean a manufactured item which, unfortunately, is the most generally understood description of the word. As has been said a product could be described as the result of one's own endeavours. Anything we do results in a product and if that product is found to be wrong, or non-conforming, then action must be taken to identify the cause of the problem and dispose of it.

Whatever the product may be, and these can be many and varied, there should be a method to identify the problem and for the notification of the people concerned.

Non-conforming products can cover such items as:

— an incorrect invoice
— a poorly serviced hotel room
— a wrongly supplied drug
— an incorrect figure on a bank statement

and so on.

The responsibility for the review and eventual correction of the problem should be defined. In the case of minor problems, these can, in all probability, be dealt with immediately but in the case of major non-conformances these should be reviewed by relevant personnel and the appropriate action taken.

(7)   CORRECTIVE ACTION

This activity follows on from section paragraph (6) above.

It should be the duty and responsibility of everyone within the service organization to identify and report on the existence of non-conformances and it is important that such non-conformances are discovered and dealt with before the customer is affected. Wherever there is a non-conformance, then action will must be taken not only to correct the deficiency but to implement action to prevent a recurrence of the problem. The action to prevent a recurrence is most important. Experience has shown that correcting a problem does not necessarily prevent it happening again. The action to prevent a recurrence could take many forms, from the issue of a reprimand, through additional training to, perhaps, the ultimate replacement of the offending person. Alternatively, it may be that the documented procedure does not reflect actual practice and will have to be amended to suit the reality.

In determining action to prevent recurrence, the economics of such action must be considered. It may well be less costly to live with the problem and rectify it each time it occurs rather than invest in very costly preventative measures. Management must make this decision, which should be documented. When implemented corrective action should be monitored to ensure its effectiveness.

In addition to correcting deficiencies observed by the organization itself, corrective action should be implemented also with regard to customer complaints. Such action should be undertaken within a specified time acceptable to the customer. Attention paid to dealing with customer complaints in an expeditious manner is the hallmark of a company which has the customer's interests at heart.

(8) RECORDS

All companies, regardless of size, product or service, will have a requirement to keep records. Unfortunately not all companies have a documented policy for record retention and, in the main, records are retained on the 'just in case' philosophy rather than the 'need' to keep such records. Management should, therefore, determine firstly the records that 'need' to be kept and secondly the retention time for such records.

Experience has shown that many organizations have considerable problems in this area. In essence, record keeping could be defined in three words: filing and finding. The filing of the records and the ability to find such records with the minimum of time and effort is, again, a hallmark of a well-organized document control system.

In the main, the records which are to be developed and maintained relate to what are described as quality-related activities. These records provide the objective evidence that a service meets customer or specification requirements and it is this objective evidence which the quality assurance auditor will seek to confirm compliance with the system.

Records would comprise such details as:

(1) system and compliance audit reports,
(2) data covering the reliability of purchasing sources,
(3) details of non-conforming services/items,
(4) details of corrective action,
(5) certification for approval of personnel.

All records should be reviewed and evaluated regularly by responsible personnel. The result of such reviews should be used for the purpose of improving and updating the quality systems.

Records should be retained for the period set by the company, by legislation or by the customer (whichever is the maximum). Records should be stored in a suitable environment which will minimize deterioration or damage and prevent loss. In normal circumstances, this should be in steel cabinets which are water-resistant and fire-retardant.

Other methods of record retention may be used, such as computerized data storage, microfilm or microfiche, but such should be agreed with the customer where necessary.

(9) INTERNAL QUALITY AUDITS

This is an activity which is very much overlooked by most companies. A company's quality system is not generally seen in the same light as the financial accounting system, yet, as has already been previously indicated, if there should be inefficient control over all its activities, a company could well be losing a great deal of money.

Quality costs have been discussed earlier in this book and it is in the detection of such costs that the quality audit, if effectively undertaken, is such a major management tool. The importance of it is such that a separate chapter is devoted to this activity (see Chapter 7).

(10)   TRAINING

This is another activity which is neglected by many companies, yet it is, again, most important. The lack of a management policy in this area can contribute significantly to quality costs.

Training can be required in many areas in the service industry, ranging from the training of secretarial personnel through to highly sophisticated training for specialized service applications. The introduction of new machinery and equipment, the upgrading of personnel to meet new employment criteria, and the retraining of operatives to take on additional responsibilities to meet the demands of new technology are just some of the areas which should be covered by a corporate training policy.

In determining training requirements, consideration should be given to those functions which require acquired skills and those functions which could be adversely affected by lack of skill. Such functions should be identified, categorized and documented.

Training should not be restricted to those with assigned quality responsibilities. For example, senior management should be educated in the principles, practices, and applications of quality management and, in particular, in evaluating and assessing quality costs; similarly, all personnel should be aware of the company's quality policy and objectives with induction and awareness programmes for new entrants.

The following is a non-exhaustive list of functions which could be considered as requiring skills which should be covered by training:

— quality management,
— auditing (internal),
— word processing,
— telephone answering,
— computing,
— hotel room servicing,
— reception services,
— radiography (health services).

Management should establish, by review, examination or other means, whether personnel carrying out such functions require training or additional experience to make good any shortfall. Management should also establish how competence in a given function is determined, by examination, testing, certification, or other means.

The methods to be used in making good such shortfall in experience or training should be documented and would include training or indoctrination by in-house training schemes or by third-party training organizations.

Records of training involvement, together with examination or test results (where applicable), should be documented and made available to the customer or regulatory body as required. Training in certain functions requires regular updating and the necessary evidence that such retraining or maintenance of qualifications has been carried out should be documented.

CONCLUSION

If the above activities are examined it will be seen that these are all applicable not only to every shape and size of company but also to every department or section within a company. They are, in essence, *the ten essential elements of* any quality management system. It stands to reason, therefore, that if such is the case then management should pay much more attention to issuing directives on how these activities are to be undertaken rather than relying on a so called 'quality department' to do it for them. After all is said and done, the purpose of a quality management system should be to improve the overall performance and efficiency of the business, which is, most definitely, a management responsibility.

6

System documentation

Say well is good but Do well is better.

Old English proverb (c. 1639).

An effective quality management system can be seen to be only as good as the documentation that controls it and it will be necessary, therefore, to describe clearly the details of the system and to communicate these details to all concerned. As has already been stated in previous chapters the documented description of the system should be developed to cover the following:

— management's policy towards quality,
— the objectives and expected benefits of the quality system,
— the organization and responsibilities of all within the company,
— operational methods.

THE NEED FOR DOCUMENTATION

The documentation will, if produced in a systematic and consistent manner, formalize the system which, in turn, should:

— demonstrate a clear and concise statement to all personnel;
— encourage consistency of action and uniformity of understanding throughout the business;
— be easily distributed;
— convey the same (consistent) message or instruction simultaneously to all appropriate personnel;
— facilitate effective management of change, revision and updating (changes being easily incorporated and approval demonstrated by means of a signature, with the notification of the change being issued to all points of use concurrently);

— ensure permanence and *reduce the learning curve* when personnel changes occur;
— assist in the monitoring of the system (informal, oral instructions cannot be verified).

Quality system documentation should not, however, be excessive and should not be synonymous with 'paper generation'. It should be well planned, simple, clear, concise and well-controlled. The object of the paperwork, believe it or not, is to make life simpler. Above all else, the documentation provides a very good check list. If the procedures are being followed, then nothing should be overlooked or left to chance. It will eliminate the 'I did not think about it' syndrome. The simple act of having to write something down clarifies the mind wonderfully.

Also, procedures are not implemented in order to find someone to blame if things go wrong; they are designed to prevent things going wrong. Furthermore, the system, if properly developed, should not allow anyone to 'pass the buck'.

THE 'TIERS' OF DOCUMENTATION

Associated with the quality system are a number of types of documentation which describe what the system is intended to achieve, how it works, what deliverables are to be produced, by whom and when. This documentation is usually given the all-embracing title of 'Work instructions' and is, generally, in the four tiers which have been described previously. To recap, these are:

Tier 1 — The quality manual, which defines the policies, objectives, organizational structures and summarizes the general quality practices of the company.

Tier 2 — Procedures, which describe what is to be done, by whom and how, when, where and why an activity is to be carried out.

Tier 3 — Job instructions, which direct personnel in a single activity and are subordinate documents to procedures. Such instructions may be required for specific tasks, processes or operations; test and/or inspection activities.

Tier 4 — Forms and records, which include files; technical, statutory and legal documents; specifications; codes of practice and all other documentation which will demonstrate the achievement of the quality system requirements.

DOCUMENTATION DEVELOPMENT

In order to develop effective quality system documentation, management will, initially, be required to identify the purpose and scope of the system and the activities which need to be procedurally controlled.

Purpose and scope
The purpose and scope of the quality system will eventually be determined by the objectives set by management and each company should decide to what degree, and to which functions, procedural development is to be applied.

The activities to be procedurally controlled
Consideration should be given to the quality (fitness for purpose) of a function, item, product or service and the efficiency with which it is to be carried out and, in determining such, an evaluation should be undertaken with regard to the implications of a failure in light of:

— the cost of putting it right,
— the time involved in putting it right,
— the resources required to put it right,
— safety.

In other words, the 'corset' analogy which was discussed earlier.

THE POLICY STATEMENT

Any declaration, such as a bill passed by Parliament, trade agreement, social contract, or similar pronouncement, becomes valid only when signed by a person, or persons, in the highest authority. Similarly, any quality management system can be considered to have any 'teeth' only if signed by the highest authority in an organization.

It will be, of course, necessary to formalize the purpose and objectives of the system into a document which is generally given a title such as 'Quality manual'. The actual development and contents of a manual will be dealt with later but there should be a signed declaration issued by the chief executive which signifies commitment to the documented system.

As with any declaration of intent, however, it can be considered to be effective only in its actual implementation. There are many instances, in all walks of life, where agreements or declarations of intent have been signed in all good faith but have been found not to be worth the paper they are written on owing to lack of implementation, caused either by the inability of the signatories to support or enforce the agreement or perhaps by a change in administration.

At least, in the quality-conscious company, the senior executive, in conjunction with his/her quality management executive, will have been instrumental in the development and implementation of the quality management system and should, therefore, be familiar with its contents.

The senior executive should, if totally committed, therefore have no hesitation in signifying this commitment by appending his or her signature to such a declaration of intent. This declaration of intent is generally known as a policy statement (which has been touched upon earlier).

The signed policy statement should give all employees and potential customers an initial indication of that company's intentions towards quality and the benefits expected from it but, in order to determine the effectiveness of the quality management system, the customer could and, in the case of government agencies, very often does undertake an assessment or audit to verify that what is documented actually happens in practice. Similarly, the senior executive maintains confidence in the implementation and effectiveness of the company's own quality management system by means of internal audits, which are carried out by an independent function — normally the quality assurance department.

A company's commitment to quality can, therefore, be judged initially by the strength of the signed policy statement and, subsequently, by management's attitude as a whole and, therefore, the extent to which it is actually put into practice. The policy statement, therefore, could be defined as:

> a signed declaration issued by the chief executive of a company signifying that company's commitment to a given quality management system.

In the author's experience, a policy statement carries much more psychological weight if it is issued on the company's official headed paper. In this format, it can then be used as a 'stand-alone' document in a variety of situations such as sales promotion, employee awareness, and others. It would be management's responsibility to ensure that this policy is understood, implemented and maintained at all levels of the business. It is not uncommon for such a statement to be prominently displayed throughout the company. In fact, in the author's experience, many companies issue this statement on a small printed 'tent' card, which is displayed on the desks of management and supervisory staff, thus serving as a constant reminder of the company's commitment to quality. An example of a typical policy statement is shown as Fig. 6.1. In addition to its prominent display thoughout the business premises this policy statement will be eventually included in the quality manual.

THE QUALITY MANUAL

The quality manual was touched upon earlier and could be described as a document setting out the general quality policies, procedures and practices of an organization.

WHY A QUALITY MANUAL IS NEEDED

In addition to the fact that most quality standards indicate the requirement for such a document, there are a number of other very good reasons for its production.

```
┌─────────────────────────────────────────────────────────────────┐
│                            The XYZ Services Company Limited       │
│                                              Acme House           │
│                                              First Street         │
│                                              Primaton             │
│                      POLICY STATEMENT                             │
│  The XYZ Services Company Limited is in the business of providing │
│  specialized services to commercial and government bodies. The    │
│  nature of the company's activities places particular emphasis upon│
│  experience, expertise, capability, reliability and quality.      │
│                                                                   │
│  The company is the world's leading services organization. We are │
│  committed to retaining this position by meeting long-term growth │
│  in demand and by providing our services in a manner which meets  │
│  customer expectations and achieves the highest level of customer │
│  satisfaction and value for money.                                │
│                                                                   │
│  A N Other                                                        │
│  Senior Executive                                                 │
│  (date)                                                           │
└─────────────────────────────────────────────────────────────────┘
```

Fig.6.1 — Typical policy statement.

It is a very good management 'tool' to keep employees aware of their responsibilities within the quality system; it can thus become a suitable training document.

Its use can reduce the 'learning curve' resulting from employee turnover and can thus assist in the continuity of events in such cases.

It can, if well-written and produced, become a useful addition to the 'sales aids' of an organization, as it will outline a company's intentions with regard to satisfying the customer by producing services and/or items which are fit for purpose, meet customer requirements and are right first time, every time.

THE SHOP WINDOW TO QUALITY

The quality manual could be described as a company's shop window to quality. It is to the company as the display window is to a store. The items in the store window will indicate to a prospective customer the nature and quality of the merchandise which the store has for sale and, in order to appreciate the totality of its stock, the customer will venture inside and purchase whatever it is that is required.

Similarly, the quality manual describes a company's intentions towards satisfying the fitness for purpose criteria and the prospective customer, as for the merchandising store, can venture inside the company and verify that company's commitment to quality by assessing or auditing the system. It would, unfortunately, be difficult for the many customers of banks, building societies, insurance companies, public bodies and the like to audit the quality management system (where one exists) of the businesses concerned but the thought does generate all sorts of enlightening situations. Perhaps the various consumer bodies could undertake audits on the consumers' behalf and publicly present the findings. The results could be quite thought-provoking!

The quality manual, therefore, states in general terms the methods used by a company to assure quality. It is, as has already been indicated, a document of intent, describing 'what' is done to assure quality. The detailed procedures, which should be available at the activity locations, will describe, in addition, the 'who', 'how', 'when', 'where' and, possibly, 'why' of an activity.

MANUAL FORMAT AND CONTENTS

There is no defined format for a manual. The presentation of the document is a matter of personal choice but, in essence, it should be designed so that it is easily updated.

All activities and functions which require to be controlled should firstly be collated into system element or procedure outlines. These outlines should describe in general terms what is required to control a given activity and it is these outlines which form the basis of a quality manual.

As a guide, it is recommended that a manual comprises three sections, as follows:

(1)   Company quality policy

— policy statement;
— statement on quality assurance authority and responsibility;
— details of company and quality assurance organization;
— statement on the manual amendments, reissue and distribution.

(2)   System element outlines

— outlines of the system's elements which address the applicable criteria of the company's quality system.

(3)   Procedures register
— a register or list of the company's procedures applicable to the quality system.

Let us take each in turn.

(1)   Company quality policy

This section should be devoted entirely to describing the company's commitment to quality and should include the following:

(a) The policy statement, which was described in detail earlier.

(b) A statement on the authority and responsibility for quality management.

This would detail the organization for quality as related to the requirements of the company, but, wherever possible, it is to be emphasized that the person appointed should have the necessary authority and responsibility to ensure that the company's quality system is being implemented and adhered to by all concerned. Such responsibility will normally mean that the person so appointed should be of management status and should be preferably independent of other functions. The quality system authority statement will describe this, and a typical statement covering such authority would read as follows:

Authority and responsibilities

Department and Function Managers

With regard to quality, all Department and Function Managers shall be responsible for:

1. The quality of work carried out by all personnel within their respective departments or functions.
2. Verifying that approved procedures are adopted within their department or function and that any necessary complementary procedures are established, implemented, reviewed and updated as required.
3. Ensuring that all staff are adequately qualified and experienced in their relevant function to perform the duties of their position in a satisfactory manner.
4. Ensuring that all staff are familiar with company procedures and have ready access to them.

Quality Management Representative

1. The Quality Management Representative is the final authority and represents the company on all matters pertinent to the quality management system as established by customer requirements, regulatory requirements and company quality policies and procedures. The Quality Management Representative reports directly to the Managing Director.
2. The Quality Management Representative has the primary responsibility to structure the quality management system, which will involve all company departments and/or functions in a focused effort to ensure compliance with quality requirements.
3. Specifically the Quality Management Representative is involved in areas such as:

— drafting company policy on quality;
— setting company quality objectives;
— reviewing the organizational relationships as they affect quality and developing proposals for improvement;
— determining and reporting the principal causes of quality losses and non-conformances;
— monitoring the company's quality management system to determine where improvements are needed and recommending, as necessary, the appropriate corrective action.

(c) The details of company and quality management organization normally comprise organization charts which show:
— The company organization with departmental/functional reporting lines. This chart should be developed to show the relationships, interfaces and hierarchical structure of the various departments or functions.
— The quality management organization with its independence from other functions.

Typical charts for both company and quality management organizations are given in Figs 6.2 and 6.3.

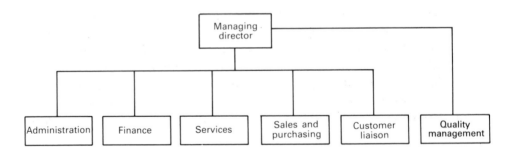

Fig. 6.2 — Company organization.

(d) The statement on amendments, reissue and distribution should indicate how amendments to the manual are dealt with. It should also indicate what is done to control the distribution of the manual.

Controlled and uncontrolled distribution
Manuals, as for most other documents, are issued under **controlled** and **uncontrolled** conditions.

Controlled conditions imply that the document is given a serial number

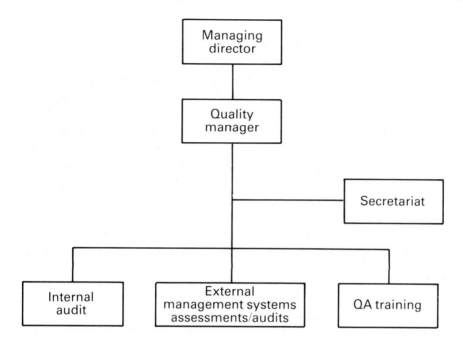

Fig. 6.3 — Quality management department organization.

and allocated to a specified person. The recipient of the document acknowledges receipt and is provided automatically with amendments and reissues.

Uncontrolled conditions imply that the document is issued for information purposes only and, as such, will not be kept updated.

It is in a company's interest to keep all document distribution to a minimum. One should establish a 'need to know' rather than a 'want to know' distribution list.

A typical statement on amendments, reissue and distribution could read as follows:

Amendments, reissue and distribution

The XYZ Service Company Limited's Quality Management Department reviews this manual periodically with other departments and functions to reaffirm its adequacy and conformance to current requirements of the XYZ Service Company Limited. The maximum period for review of the manual is one year.

Amendments to the manual are made as required to reflect the current quality management system. The amendments are made by replacement of the applicable page(s). Each amended page is identified by amendment number and date of amendment.

Amendments are numbered consecutively until such time as a new edition incorporates all such changes. When changes affect a considerable number of pages, and in any case after not more than ten amendments to one edition, the manual is reissued as a new edition. Editions are identified in alphabetical sequence. Each edition cancels and replaces all previous editions and amendments. The amendment list indicates all the amendments to the latest edition of the manual.

A complete list of quality management manual holders, together with the amendment records, is retained by the . . . (here would be inserted the department responsible for the function, i.e. Quality Management Department, Document Control Department, Library, or others). Amendments and new editions of the manual are automatically distributed to all registered holders.

It shall be the responsibility of all registered manual holders to update the manual assigned to them and destroy obsolete copies of all amended pages.

(2) System element outlines

This section should contain brief outlines of the primary functions of the company's quality management system as determined by both company and customer requirements.

It should include the controls to be exercised on those aspects of the function which have an effect on quality to ensure conformance to customer needs (stated or implied). The elements outlined should reflect not only current quality policies but should also take into consideration, where applicable, the requirements of any pertinent national and/or international standards and regulations relating to quality management systems.

Unless the company is very small with few functional controls, the inclusion of detailed procedures within a manual is to be avoided. There are three very good reasons for this:

(1) Procedures are 'living' documents and are continually under review. Experience has shown that a procedure cannot be considered to have attained its full 'maturity' with regard to content, acceptability and effectiveness until it has reached revision four. If procedures are included in the manual, updating becomes a very costly and laborious process. If, however, procedures are kept separate from the manual, then any procedural amendments would be an independent exercise which would have no effect on the outlines in the manual.

(2) The majority of the recipients of a manual would not generally be concerned with the detailed aspects of a given activity or the technicalities of its operation. Detailed procedures would, therefore, be just additional pieces of paper for which they will have no use.

(3) Procedures are proprietary documents which have taken a great deal of

time and effort to produce. They are for company use only and should not be made freely available to third parties. Procedures should generally be made available only to those who are to implement them.

There is, of course, the inevitable exception to the rule. When procedures are developed to meet certain specified customer requirements, the customer will invariably wish to review them to determine their compliance with specific contract conditions. The system element outlines should follow a logical sequence and should cover all aspects of the relevant criteria of the company's quality system.

A typical index of the system's elements outlines would include the *essential elements* plus other elements as appropriate to the business. Outlines for the essential elements are given as appendix A to this book.

(3)   Procedures register

This section should include a list of the procedures for all the activities and functions applicable to a company's quality management system.

While it is generally necessary to include only those procedures which support the system, it is worthwhile listing the procedures which relate to all management functions. Such a list will then assist company personnel in determining the correct procedure for any given function.

The information enumerated in this section should include the document title with the relevant document number. The author does not recommend the inclusion of procedure revision status as this can lead only to unnecessary updating of this section. Procedure revisions should be controlled by the responsible department. Procedures, as for any document, should carry an identification number to facilitate control. A typical numbering sequence for procedures would be the tripartite system as follows:

XYZ–MAN–001

In this example, the company's identity is represented by the first three letters (in this case the XYZ Service Company Limited). The department or function is represented by the second set of three (in this case MAN refers to Management) and finally the three digits refer to the procedure number.

The following is a typical, but by no means exhaustive, procedures index:

MANAGEMENT AND ADMINISTRATION
Sales and marketing	XYZ-MAN-001
Public relations	XYZ-MAN-002
Review of quality system	XYZ-MAN-003
Communications	XYZ-MAN-004
Safety policy	XYZ-MAN-005
Contract control	XYZ-MAN-006

| Minutes of meetings | XYZ-MAN-007 |
| Personnel training | XYZ-MAN-008 |

and others.

DOCUMENT CONTROL

Document numbering and identification	XYZ-DOC-001
Procedures preparation — style and format	XYZ-DOC-002
Development, approval and implementation of activity documents	XYZ-DOC-003
Procedures register	XYZ-DOC-004
Document storage and retrieval	XYZ-DOC-005
Operating manuals and dossiers	XYZ-DOC-006
Records/certification	XYZ-DOC-007
Document revision and distribution	XYZ-DOC-008

and others.

PLANNING

Contract review meetings	XYZ-PLA-001
Progress reporting	XYZ-PLA-002
Work activity packages	XYZ-PLA-003

and others.

PROCUREMENT

Vendor assessment	XYZ-PRO-001
Tender package development	XYZ-PRO-002
Bid package review and evaluation	XYZ-PRO-003
Supplier selection	XYZ-PRO-004
Purchase orders	XYZ-PRO-005
Expediting	XYZ-PRO-006

and others.

QUALITY MANAGEMENT

Quality manual	XYZ-QM-001
Audits — internal/external	XYZ-QM-002
Audits — extrinsic	XYZ-QM-003
Corrective action request	XYZ-QM-004
Auditor qualification and training	XYZ-QM-005

and others.

As can be seen from the above, when procedures are related to the function they are intended to control, very few are actually the responsibility of the quality management function or department. In many organizations, all procedures are regarded as quality management procedures, which can only confirm the lack of understanding of quality management concepts. In summary, one should endeavour to keep the manual simple. It is, as has already been emphasized, a document of intent.

The inclusion of any information which is likely to be subject to continual amendment should be avoided. Procedures are one example of details not to be included; organization charts are another. It is recommended that titles or functions, and not the individuals' names, be indicated on such charts. Titles or functions, once established, do not normally change but individuals most certainly do!

PROCEDURE DEVELOPMENT, ADMINISTRATION AND CONTROL

Now that the system outlines have been developed and incorporated into the quality manual, the next step is to produce the detailed procedures. Procedures, as has been said, comprise the real evidence of quality and should be considered mandatory for any quality management system.

In order to document any activity, one must understand how that activity is carried out and how each step within a given activity leads into the next step. When documenting any activity the actual act of writing it down can highlight such matters as anomalies, duplications, lack of important interfaces, and other possible deficiencies.

The understanding of how each activity is carried out must point to the fact that procedures can be considered as representing a true account of an activity only if the personnel actually carrying out that activity are involved with the procedure development.

It also goes without saying that once an activity is 'proceduralized' it facilitates review by others who may have an involvement in that activity and any changes in the activity will be automatically documented. Documented changes will highlight to all concerned at the same time that such a change has been made. Documented changes will also act as an audit trail in the event of information being required at a later date to verify when and why an activity was amended. Procedures will also assist in reducing the 'learning curve' when employee changes are made.

As has been said, procedures should define the purpose and scope of an activity and specify what is to be done, by whom, and how, when, where and why an activity is to be carried out.

Procedures will ensure that controls operate consistently and effectively, that people communicate and that events occur in a planned and systematic manner. They are not meant to be detailed instructions for controlling individual processes or activities; such would normally be described in job instructions which are, in turn, referenced by procedures. This would apply equally to activities which could be considered as being 'external' to the company's operations, yet which are very much the company's responsibility, such as instructions for servicing equipment at site and codes of practice.

The development of procedures is a major activity in itself and should therefore be planned and co-ordinated with the groups of people involved. The planning and subsequent development of procedures will require consideration of the following:

— who writes them (responsibilities),
— how they will be planned and developed,
— how they are to be written and presented,
— how they are to be identified,
— who will control them and how.

In the following sections each of these aspects is dealt with in more detail.

There are several key issues in procedure administration and control which should be determined before the preparation of procedures can begin, and all should be finalized before procedures are issued. These are:

— the definition of responsibilities,
— the procedure numbering system,
— methods of procedure amendment and revision,
— methods of controlling distribution.

DEFINITION OF RESPONSIBILITIES

There are three primary areas of responsibility regarding procedure development which should be defined. These are:

(1) identification, review and authorization.
(2) preparation (writing),
(3) administration and control.

Identification, review and authorization

Normally, management is responsible for identifying the need for a new procedure or set of procedures based upon the activities of the organization concerned.

Once written, procedures should be reviewed at both departmental and functional levels to ensure that:

— any conflicts within, or between, existing procedures are identified and resolved
— procedures reflect current practice and provide adequate direction
— interfaces are defined and agreed at both departmental and functional levels.

Ultimately, to become an official corporate document, the procedure should be approved by an authorized or nominated signatory. A procedure may require approval from any or all of the following personnel:

— departmental head or manager,
— quality manager,
— managing director.

Management will make this decision, which in itself, should be documented and updated as necessary.

Preparation (writing)
Utilizing the agreed structure or format, procedure writing should be undertaken by personnel who are familiar with the activities and functions to be controlled. This responsibility should not be placed upon the quality department (although this department may offer guidance on the format to be adopted). It will be necessary, therefore, to nominate an author or authors.

Administration and control
Management should determine the methods of, and the responsibilities for, the administration and control of procedures, including such issues as:

— the format in which procedures are to be written;
— the numbering system to be followed;
— the system for review;
— the methods to be followed for approval, amendment and revision;
— storage, distribution and retrieval.

PROCEDURE NUMBERING SYSTEM

A procedure numbering system should be developed. This system should allow adequate facility for expansion (i.e. the inclusion of new procedures) and should convey some meaning to the reader. A typical procedure numbering system has already been indicated earlier in this chapter but whatever method is used it should be consistent with existing corporate or divisional systems.

Forms also should be numbered so that they can be traced to the procedure that generates them. For example, a form identified as attachment 6.1 of, say, procedure XYZ-MAN-001 would be numbered MAN-0011, attachment 6.2 would be numbered MAN-0012 and so on.

PROCEDURE AMENDMENT AND REVISION

As a quality system is continually subject to review and improvement, the procedures themselves become active or dynamic documents and, from time to time, will require amendment or revision. In this respect, there are several important points to consider, namely:

— revision status,
— revision identification,
— revision record,
— revision edition.

Revision status

Each page of the procedure should be identified with the revision status and date. Revision status indicators generally follow a numeric system commencing at 0 and proceeding through 1, 2, 3 and onwards as required. Revision 0 is generally utilized for the 'issued for comment' stage.

Revision identification

The extent of the revision made should be indicated within the text of the document. This is usually undertaken by stating the revision number in parentheses in the margin with a line extending down to the end of the text revised, thus:

$$\Big| [2]$$

Revision record

In order to determine that one is in possession of the latest revision of a procedure, it is considered good practice to include a record of revisions on the front of the document, or at the front of a manual containing a set of procedures.

This record of revisions can be indicated by means of a revision record box on the front sheet of the procedure or by means of an amendment or revision record register immediately inside the cover page.

As a minimum, the revision status indicator should identify:

— the revision status (e.g. 0, 1, 2, 3)
— the date of the revision
— the pages/procedures affected by the revision
— authorization for revision.

It is important that the department which is responsible for document control maintains a master index of revisions to all procedures — an index that has itself a revision number and date for traceability.

Issuing revised documentation

There are variations in the methods by which different organizations issue procedure revisions. Some companies favour the reissue of the entire document at every revision. Others issue only the affected pages until such time as a major revision is undertaken which, in order to avoid confusion, will necessitate the complete document being reissued as a new edition. When new editions are produced, it is usual to classify them with some form of identification. As for the manual, an alphabetical sequence is generally used for this purpose.

The safest approach is to reissue the entire procedure each time it is revised. This, however, is more costly and time-consuming but is generally easier to control. Holders of procedures manuals are more likely to replace complete documents than to replace individual pages.

Revisions should be issued to all holders of the procedure or procedures manual under the cover of a transmittal memorandum or letter. This transmittal memorandum/letter (as was discussed in Chapter 5) should provide for the receiver to acknowledge not only receipt of the amended document but also to signify the incorporation of the revision in their procedure manual and the disposal of the superseded document/page(s). A copy of the transmittal document is then returned to the document control function.

DISTRIBUTION CONTROL

Document distribution should be developed on a *need to know* rather than a *want to know* basis and should be planned, formalized and controlled with clearly defined responsibilities. Procedures may be in the form of individual documents, a bound manual, or a series of manuals. These are controlled copies, i.e. each procedure or manual is numbered and signed out to, and receipted by, a nominated individual.

Periodic audits should be undertaken to verify that copies are kept up to date, with all latest revisions incorporated and superseded versions or unofficial copies destroyed.

Unauthorized copying of documents should be discouraged by means of a document control system which clearly identifies those personnel who are responsible for document reproduction and also the method used to classify 'controlled copies'.

PROCEDURE PRESENTATION

Finally, management should determine how procedures are to be prepared, presented, printed and distributed. All personnel concerned with procedure development should be made aware of such directives.

Due consideration should, therefore, be given to:

— the use of word processing equipment and software
— the format, font size, typeface, character facing and methods of presentation
— the methods of reproduction such as photocopying or offset printing
— the use of special paper.

PROCEDURE PLANNING AND DEVELOPMENT

Development of the full register of procedures is the responsibility of management and should be addressed during the planning stage of the quality system.

The development of individual procedures, however, will be the responsibility of the nominated author(s) and will require careful planning.

PROCEDURE PLANNING

Planning is an essential part of procedure development and if undertaken systematically will assist in the production of logical, well-structured and coherent documents.

Procedure planning involves establishing firstly the scope of the activity to be addressed by the procedure and secondly the objectives of the control of that activity.

Scope

The scope of an activity which is to be addressed by an individual procedure will be dependent upon a number of criteria such as:

— the nature of the activity which is to be controlled;
— the interfaces with other related activities and hence other procedures;
— the amount of manageable information, or instructions, which can be covered by the document.

Objectives

The objectives for the control of an activity should be determined by management and, where possible, the achievement of specified objectives should be verifiable by measurement.

PROCEDURE DEVELOPMENT

Experience has shown that there are ten distinct steps to be taken in developing procedures. These are:

(1) Review current practice.
(2) Analyse current practice.
(3) Develop a draft procedure.
(4) Release draft for comment.
(5) Review comments.
(6) Revise and issue procedure for acceptance.
(7) Obtain approval.

(8) Issue for use.
(9) Implement.
(10) Monitor and review.

Review current practice
This will involve discussions with other people concerned and will include a review of all existing applicable documentation, procedures and instructions. It will then be necessary to:

— verify and record the current routine methods of performing an activity;
— identify responsibilities, documentation and equipment used to undertake the activity;
— determine the current standards (acceptance criteria), if any, which are applied and how effectively they are being utilized;
— identify those aspects of an activity which significantly impact on quality.

Analyse current practice
An analysis of current practice should be undertaken in conjunction with all involved personnel to verify whether such practices are indeed satisfactory and whether any changes need to be made. As a result of such an analysis it should be possible to:

— confirm that the specified objectives are currently being achieved;
— agree on the best methods of achieving the required levels of quality;
— identify any gaps, duplications or areas of weakness, especially with regard to communication problems between departments and/or functions;
— verify potential areas for improvement.

Develop a draft procedure
A draft document should be initiated which formulates the method by which an activity is (or is to be) carried out, indicating who does what, how, when, where and why. The procedure itself should be developed to an agreed format. The subject of format is discussed later in this chapter.

An effective way of logically ordering the steps of an activity is to outline them utilizing flow chart techniques. A great deal has been written on flow charting and it is not necessary to go through these in detail here. However, Fig. 6.4 indicates some typical flowcharting symbols which can be used for this purpose.

In order to flow chart an activity and to develop an effective procedure, it is important to indicate how each activity is carried out, how each step is initiated and how it leads into the next. Information and instructions on how each step is conducted should be easy to follow. The process of documenting

Initiation of a document

An activity or operation

A decision must be made

Documents are filed

Terminator – final activity

Fig. 6.4 — Some typical flowcharting symbols.

current practice may uncover a potential for change and improvement in methods.

Only instructions which are specific to the scope of the particular activity which is to be controlled should be included in the procedure. These should be clearly defined by means of 'purpose' and 'scope' statements. References, or interfaces with related documents, should be included where appropriate. In some instances, if there is too much information to be contained in a single document, more than one procedure may be required. Where possible, try to avoid wide variations in procedure length.

The degree of detail required in describing various steps/instructions will be dependent upon the personnel for whom the procedure is being written and the level of training or experience of such personnel.

One of the most important items to be determined when considering a documented instruction, or the need for such an instruction, is the effect this instruction may have on the performance of the work.

The ultimate test of any procedure is in its ability to provide the control to achieve the result for which it was developed. Where relevant, the procedure should make reference to 'tier 3' or tier '4' documents, as appropriate. The procedure is not intended to *replace* detailed job instructions but to support them. Likewise, the development of a procedure may actually require that certain documents, e.g. 'tier 4' forms and records, be designed to ensure adequate control.

Release draft for comment

Once developed, the draft procedure should be designated as revision 0 (issued for comment) and distributed to all involved personnel for their review with some indication of when the document is to be returned to the originator. Alternatively a default instruction could be issued which would read 'if comments are not received by such and such a date it will be assumed that the recipient has no comment to make'. Experience has shown that reviews of this kind can extend the document development schedule if no deadline is indicated. Management must support such a ruling.

Review comments

The comments should then be reviewed to determine which are applicable and which are required to be incorporated in the document. Any amendments agreed at this stage should be recorded.

Revise and issue procedure for acceptance

Incorporate those amendments which are considered appropriate and re-issue the document for approval.

Obtain approval

The procedure should then be checked by the responsible nominated person and approved by management prior to issue for use.

Issue for use

The document would then be formally issued as revision 1 (issued for use) and distributed to all relevant locations in accordance with the agreed distribution instructions. Issue does not necessarily imply that all concerned should receive an individual copy. In instances where a number of people will use the same procedure, then 'ready access' to the procedure should be sufficient. Procedures, as for the quality manual, should be issued under controlled or uncontrolled conditions.

Implement
The implementation of a procedure should include an element of instruction so that all involved personnel are familiar with the content and methods of application.

Monitor and review
After a few weeks of application, the procedure should be audited to verify implementation, effectiveness and adherence. Should the audit indicate a lack of adherence then corrective action should be undertaken to correct and prevent a recurrence of the deficiency. It may well be that the procedure itself does not truly represent actual practice, in which case it should be revised, which would entail a revision 2 (amended as indicated). On the other hand it may well be that the person involved is not adhering to the procedure, owing to a variety of reasons, in which case action would be taken to rectify the problem (retraining, awareness or perhaps more drastic measures).

PROCEDURAL FLEXIBILITY
In the final analysis, a procedure is issued to direct people in executing an activity. Whereas it is possible to instruct members of one's own workforce, it is virtually impossible to involve others outside the workplace. Do not, therefore, include in a procedure any activity over which one has no direct control. For example, in a procedure issued by a company there was an instruction for all documentation issued to Client for approval to be routed through the document control section. The procedure also instructed that, after approval, the client shall route documents via the document control section to the originator. In most cases this instruction was not complied with and the documents were returned by the client direct to the originator. This meant that document control had no record of their return. The audit process could not include the client as an auditee, therefore the procedure should not have included an instruction on the client. The end result was to revise the method by which details of incoming documents were advised to document control.

Similarly, do not include in a procedure any instruction to which one cannot always be expected to adhere and, within reason, some flexibility should be permitted. For example, an instruction to undertake an activity in a given time — say within seven days — may not be feasible during periods where there are many public holidays. The procedure should be flexible enough to accommodate such eventualities. Always ask the question — can this instruction be adequately complied with at all times?

PROCEDURE STRUCTURE AND FORMAT

To be effective, procedures should be consistent in their presentation and uniform in their structure. Management should develop guidelines for their preparation, review and approval. Although procedure format is a matter of personal choice, experience has shown the following six section format to be effective:

    Section 1 — Purpose
    Section 2 — Scope
    Section 3 — References
    Section 4 — Definitions
    Section 5 — Actions
    Section 6 — Documentation

It is strongly recommended that, when documenting an activity, the future imperative 'shall' rather than 'will' is used in the third person. This stresses the importance of the activity and that it is to be carried out without exception. 'Shall' is mandatory, 'will' signifies an intention and, as is well known, 'The road to hell is paved with good intentions'.

CONSISTENCY

Consistency of presentation can be achieved by using:

— standard pre-printed forms,
— uniformity of presentation.

Standard forms

It is useful for procedures to be produced on pre-printed forms which provide for the inclusion of some, or all, of the following data:

— the company's name, division or logo
— the title of the document,
— the document number,
— the revision status and date.

Uniformity of presentation

For ease of reference, procedures should have a standard format. For example:

— the cover page should be identified always as page 1 and carry the
following information:
   — the procedure number,
   — the procedure title,
   — the approval authority,
   — revision/edition status
— page 2 of a procedure should contain the contents list.

Numbering of pages and the structure and numbering of paragraphs should
be consistent.

CONTENTS

Utilizing the agreed format, which in this case would be the six-section
format, as indicated above, the contents would be as follows:

Purpose

This section would outline the objectives or intention of the document. For
example, if a procedure is being written for staff recruitment, then this
section could read as follows.

> The purpose of this procedure is to define the steps to be taken in the
> recruitment of personnel to the company, ensure that those recruited
> meet requirements as advertised, and ensure that company personnel
> involved in recruitment are aware of their authority and responsibili-
> ties in this respect.

It is however important to remember that the wider the scope of the
document, the more complicated the document could become. In the above
example the scope relates to the recruitment of 'staff'. In a particular context
'staff' could cover any and every type of position related to the business. It
may be prudent, therefore, to designate the type of staff to which one is
referring, as requirements for different levels or grades of staff could differ
depending on the company's activities. For example, professional staff,
administrative or clerical staff, computing staff, nursing staff and others.

Scope

This section would outline the function, department, or group to which the
procedure applies, i.e. it defines the limits of control for each procedure.
Again using staff recruitment as an example, the scope could read:

> This procedure is applicable to all individuals engaged in the recruit-

ment of personnel to the company and covers all related activities concerned with the selection and recruitment of staff up to commencement on payroll.

References

This section would list all other documents which have a bearing on the activities and which are discussed or referred to within the body of the procedure itself. Such documents could include associated procedures, job instructions, legislative directives, national standards and specifications. In this recruitment example, these references could include such details as educational and experience requirements, statutory requirements, salary level indicators, and advertising methods.

Definitions

This section would include definitions of all words, acronyms, initials and abbreviations not generally understood by the reader. It may include the definition of words which have a specific meaning within a particular context. Where relevant, this section may make reference to associated 'quality' definitions in national standards.

Using the example above, this section could include such initials as:

> PRM — Personnel Recruitment Manager
> PRO — Personnel Recruitment Officer

Actions

This section would detail the actual instructions to be followed in undertaking the activity, stating who does what, how, when, where and why. A flow chart could be used for clarification purposes.

The effectiveness of a procedure can be determined by taking each clause of this section to see if it will turn easily into a question. This is an aid to auditing. For example, using the recruitment procedure once again, there may be a clause which reads:

Internal notification of vacancy

On instructions from the PRM, the PRO shall prepare an internal vacancy notification form (attachment 6.1). This shall include as a minimum:

— job title
— description of responsibilities
— grade/salary scale
— reporting route.

Other additional information may be included, e.g. ability to travel, driving licence essential, fluency in a foreign language.

The completed internal vacancy notification form shall be displayed on all internal notice boards (for the period defined by the PRM).

One could verify implementation by asking whether all these activities had been carried out and by the designated personnel.

Documentation
This section would list any documentation referred to within the procedure and generated as a result of implementing the procedure. A copy or example of each such document should be attached. As has already been said, it facilitates control if all documents which are generated by a given procedure carry a reference number which traces that document to the procedure. To further qualify this, it could be assumed that the procedure under discussion carries the number XYZ-PER-001; then any supporting forms would be numbered PER-0011, PER-0012 and so on.

General
It is important that the procedure content should always follow the same format without variation. In the event that, for example, there are no references, then under the section entitled References in the procedure the word NONE should be inserted. There is nothing worse than producing similar documents each with the content in a different order.

For reference and development purposes, an example of a typical procedure for writing procedures 'Procedures — preparation, style and format' is given as Appendix B to this book.

ALTERNATIVE STRUCTURES

Other possible variations on the above format are:

— 'introduction' could replace 'purpose'
— 'responsibilities' could be identified in a separate section
— 'appendices' could be listed and attached as a separate section.

Let us examine these alternatives:

Introduction
This would be the same as 'purpose' but could also reference and quote the relevant requirement of an appropriate quality system standard.

Responsibilities
This section would define who is responsible for each activity outlined in the procedure. In our recruitment example, this may be as follows:

Title:	**Personnel Recruitment Manager**
Responsibility:	Overall responsibility for the recruitment and selection of staff, in line with corporate manpower requirements and type and level of skills required.
Title:	**Personnel Recruitment Officer**
Responsibility:	The design and publication of advertisements for staff recruitment and the interviewing and assessment of potential candidates, including sourcing and filing of relevant references and related documents.

Experience has shown that, generally, most of the information detailed in a 'Responsibility' section would be repeated in the 'Actions' section of the procedure. A separate section covering responsibilities could therefore be considered as superfluous and paper-generating.

Appendices

Appendices would include any documents (e.g. supplementary or explanatory notes, organization charts, flow charts, etc.) which are distinct from the main procedure but need to be included for reference.

For example, in the recruitment procedure it may include:

(1) List of locations of all internal notice boards on which vacancies are to be advertised.
(2) List of external publications in which vacancies are to be advertised.

PROCEDURE WRITING

Before leaving the subject of the procedure, it is worthwhile looking into an effective procedure writing style. The ability to put words on to paper so that the result is clear and precise is as important as the contents of the procedure.

The objective of a procedure is to give clear guidance and direction to the reader on the nature of the activity which is to be controlled; how, when, where and by whom such an activity is to be carried out; and where interfaces occur with other related activities. It is important, therefore, to use simple and direct words and to avoid the use of the passive tense and obsolete terms.

Effective writing

Effective writing should be clear, simple and direct. Always make a point of writing for the reader and not for yourself. If the reader has problems in interpreting an instruction, or has difficulty in finding a particular point, then the procedure has not achieved its objective. In such cases, both the writer and the reader have wasted time.

Punctuation

Punctuation is an important part of clear writing and, hence, understanding. Long sentences are generally difficult to comprehend and tend to confuse the reader. It is recommended that sentences and paragraphs be kept as short as possible. In general, the principle is to keep to one instruction per sentence and one theme to a paragraph.

Use of words

Precise wording is very important in procedure writing. Use words or phrases that have specific meanings rather than words or phrases which could be open to interpretation.

Initials, acronyms and abbreviations

Initials, acronyms and abbreviations have become all too commonplace in recent years and, in many instances, can convey different meanings to different industries. It is recommended, therefore, to refrain from using them where they have multiple meanings and to avoid completely their use if they are to occur only once or twice in the procedure. If it should be necessary to use initials, acronyms or abbreviations, because of the multiplicity of occurrences, then such should be listed, together with their full meaning, in the 'Definitions' section of the procedure.

Clarity

Long or little-used words, together with long rambling sentences, cause problems when implementing procedures. They also present difficulties when auditing. It is possible to measure how clear one's writing is by means of a clarity index (sometimes referred to as a readability index). This is by no means a precise method of measurement but it is a simple aid to clarity.

This index works as follows:

(1) Choose a section of script containing about 200 words. Disregard titles and headings.
(2) Count the major punctuation marks — full stops, question marks and exclamation marks.
(3) Divide the number of such major punctuation marks into the total number of words. This will result in the average sentence length. Record this number.
(4) Underline all words of three syllables or more. Exclude proper nouns or two-syllable words that become three syllables by the addition of a prefix or suffix, such as *un*helpful, *im*polite, expect*ed*, appoint*ed*.
(5) Determine the percentage of long words. In a 200 word sample, forty long words would equate to twenty per cent. Record this percentage.

To arrive at the clarity index, add the average sentence length to the percentage of long words. If the result is below twenty, then the text is probably too abrupt. Over forty indicates there could be difficulties with interpretation.

During an average conversation most people subconsciously use an index of about thirty; the average index of newspaper articles on any one day is also about thirty.

As a guideline, if the script is written for the reader and if one writes as one speaks, then the index should be about thirty. There are limitations in the use of this index but it does provide a quick check on the clarity of one's writing. At the end of the day, it all comes down to one word:

K I S S

Keep It Sweet and Simple.

7

The quality audit

Leave no rubs nor botches in the work.

William Shakespeare, *Macbeth.*

Formal systematic audits are an integral part of any quality management system and should be carried out periodically to verify the implementation and effectiveness of the quality system and, where applicable, customer service requirements.

Although what follows is generally more appropriate to large organizations, the principles and practices of the audit process are applicable to all businesses and the same considerations must apply. The difference is simply one of scale.

Once a quality management system has been established and implemented the only possible way any business can verify the effectiveness of the system is to carry out regular internal audits. It will be necessary, therefore, to develop a capability to manage the entire process. This audit function should be independent from, and have no direct responsibility for, the implementation of the system elements.

Generally the term 'audit' is used to indicate an internal activity or an external post-contract award activity. There is, however, another term which is employed in connection with the audit process and that is 'assessment', which is used to identify an activity carried out, prior to the placement of a contract, to evaluate a potential supplier's capability. For simplicity's sake, however, the term 'audit' will be used throughout.

This chapter will deal in a general way with both the internal and external activities. It is appreciated, however, that external audit activities, in both pre- and post-contract situations, will not be applicable to all service organizations but due consideration should be given to this process.

AUDIT OBJECTIVES

In the case of the internal quality audit, the objectives of such an activity would be to:

— determine the implementation and effectiveness of one's own quality system,
— determine conformance or non-conformance of quality system elements to specified customer requirements,
— provide a basis for improvement of a quality system,
— meet regulatory requirements,
— achieve second or third party registration.

The objectives of an external audit would be to:

— evaluate a potential supplier with a view to establishing a contractual relationship,
— verify that a supplier's quality system continues to meet specified requirements and is being effectively implemented.

THE RESPONSIBILITY FOR AUDITING

As mentioned previously, it has been emphasized that one of the responsibilities of the quality assurance department or function is to undertake internal or external audits but it should be made clear to all concerned that any such audits should not result in transferring the responsibility for the achievement of quality from operating staff to the auditing function.

In the very small organization, the responsibility for auditing may rest with the senior executive. After all, as has been said many times, the senior executive has the ultimate responsibility for quality and the quality systems have been developed by him/her in conjunction with the company's senior management and, therefore, he/she should be aware of the efficiency of the organization.

WHY AUDIT?

As has been stated, there is a requirement for a company to be aware of its financial status and an audit is carried out to verify that a company's accounting system is in order and that the results are accurate. With a financial audit, however, this is undertaken as a legal requirement under the Companies Act. The results do identify a company's profit and loss position and a company's board of directors will act on the results. The 'bottom line' is the spur.

Unfortunately, a company's quality system is not generally seen in the same light as the financial accounting system, yet, if there should be inefficient control over all its activities, a company could well be losing a great deal of money. The inefficiencies due to duplication of activities, high rework and reject rates, malpractices and so on may result in the quality costs (the costs of putting things right) being higher than the overall profit margin.

A quality audit, if effectively undertaken, should uncover such problems, providing the audit is carried out against documented requirements and by trained and qualified personnel.

WHAT IS AN AUDIT?

All quality system standards call up a requirement for the auditing or the review of the quality system and, in general, such an activity could be defined as:

> A planned and documented independent activity performed in accordance with written procedures and check-lists to verify by investigation, and the examination and evaluation of objective evidence, that applicable elements of a quality system have been developed, documented and effectively implemented in accordance with specified requirements.

The ISO 8402 (Quality — vocabulary) definition is as follows:

> A systematic and independent examination to determine whether quality activities and related results comply with planned arrangements and whether these arrangements are implemented effectively and are suitable to achieve objectives.

AUDIT DEPTH, SCOPE AND TYPE

As defined above, there is a requirement to seek objective evidence to determine that an activity has been carried out in accordance with specified requirements. These specified requirements are the procedures and job instructions. Initially, however, immediately after the implementation of a quality system, an audit should be carried out to confirm that all the relevant procedures and instructions of the current revision are available at the activity locations and that personnel are aware of their responsibilities within the system. In businesses where services are undertaken on a contract basis this audit would be carried at the commencement of each contract. The objectives of such an audit would be to confirm the existence and validity of the necessary quality system elements applicable to that contract. Such an audit is known generally as a system audit.

Depth of audit

The system audit is, therefore, a superficial or 'shallow' audit and can be utilized very effectively to get the 'feel' of a quality system.

In order to confirm whether or not a procedure or job instruction is actually being implemented and is effective, an 'adherence' or 'compliance' audit is carried out (Fig. 7.1). This 'adherence' or 'compliance' audit is a 'deep' audit. It gets down to the nitty-gritty so to speak.

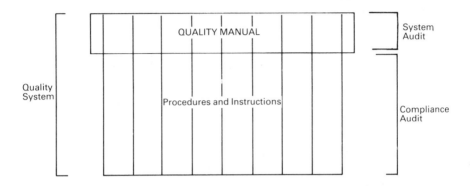

Fig. 7.1.

Scope of audit

The 'scope' of an audit relates to the amount of the quality system that should be reviewed to confirm that the activities are in compliance with requirements.

In the case of an internal activity, management, together with the quality function, will determine which quality system elements, procedures and instructions are to be audited within a given time-scale. Externally, the purchaser will make this decision. In any event, the auditee should be consulted when determining the scope of the audit.

Type of audit

The scope and depth of an audit are variable factors which have to be considered in detail during the preparation and planning of audits. The type of audit is determined by who is carrying out the audit and the location of the auditee, and can be either an internal, external or extrinsic audit.

An **internal audit** is an audit carried out by a company to evaluate its own performance. The notification procedure and the conduct of the audit are not quite as formal as for an external audit.

An **external audit** is an audit carried out by a company to evaluate the activities of its contractors, suppliers, agents, licensees, etc. The notification procedure and procedure for the conduct of the audit are more formal and necessitate more planning and preparation than for the internal audit.

An **extrinsic audit** is an audit carried out by a customer, third party organization, regulatory authority, etc., on a company to assess its activities against specific requirements. It is an audit carried out by external sources on your own organization. An extrinsic audit would normally not be addressed by an audit procedure but by a job instruction, which should describe how the company will deal with such an audit. Such a job instruction could well include:

— the requirement to advise relevant employees of the objectives and scope of the audit
— the appointment of suitable members of staff to accompany members of the audit team (generally known as escorts);
— the provision of resources for the audit team (office accommodation, telephone, copy facilities and others);
— the requirement to provide access to facilities and objective evidence as requested by the audit team members;
— the requirement to co-operate with the audit team members to permit the audit objectives to be achieved;
— the necessity to determine and implement corrective action based on the audit results.

This job instruction would, of course, indicate who in the organization would be responsible for initiating the above actions.

AUDIT SCHEDULING

The need for an audit should be determined taking into account the maturity of the system, specified or regulatory requirements and any other pertinent factors.

In the case of external audits, significant changes in management, organization, policies, techniques or technologies could well affect the system and would need to be verified. Changes to the system itself and the results of previous audits are other circumstances which should be considered when deciding audit frequency.

Internally, audits are organized on a regular basis to verify the implementation and effectiveness of one's own system and to review the results of any significant changes as described above.

In both the external and internal situations it is important to establish an audit schedule.

The audit schedule

This should be established as soon as possible after a quality system is implemented. It is recommended that a system audit be undertaken within four to six weeks of implementation and then compliance audits scheduled to commence immediately thereafter. The system audit could identify areas of concern, which should be used to establish priorities for future audits. A typical schedule is given as Fig. 7.2. This schedule can be utilized for both internal and external activities.

THE AUDIT PROCESS

Audits, like most other activities, require considerable preparation and planning, which should take into consideration the following:

— the scope and objectives of the audit;
— the identification of the auditee's personnel who have significant responsibilities regarding the scope and objectives;
— the identification of reference documents such as the applicable quality system standard, quality manual, procedures, job instructions, customer service requirements and others;
— the identification of audit team members;
— the place, date and time where the audit is to be conducted;
— the identification of the organizational functions, or system elements, to be audited;
— the anticipated time and duration for each activity;
— the development of check-lists;
— the format and distribution of the audit report.

The total audit process could, therefore, be considered as having four distinct phases, which are:

— preparation and planning,
— performance,
— reporting,
— follow-up.

Let us take each in turn.

PREPARATION AND PLANNING

This phase of the audit process is itself divided into six subsidiary activities as follows;

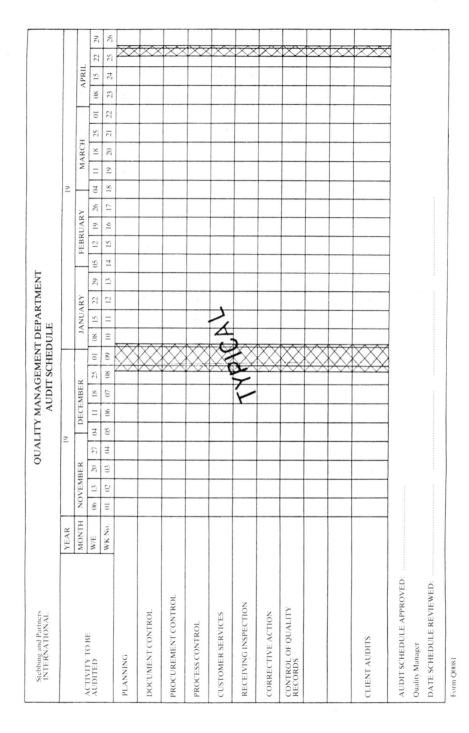

Fig. 7.2 — Typical audit schedule.

(1) Appoint a person or persons to be responsible for the audit.
(2) Notify the auditee.
(3) Agree the audit timetable.
(4) Identify, obtain and review all relevant documentation.
(5) Brief the audit team members.
(6) Develop an audit check-list.

A review of each of these activities is to be considered in detail:

(1) Appoint a person or persons to be responsible for the audit
About two weeks before a scheduled audit, the quality manager should formally assign a person to be responsible for the entire process. This person is normally a member of the quality assurance function and may even be the quality manager himself. The auditor would be advised of the date scheduled for the audit, the organization, department, function or activity to be audited, the names of the persons to contact and the scope and objectives of the audit.

Once nominated, the auditor becomes responsible for planning, preparing, performing and reporting the audit. Should the scope of the audit necessitate the use of more than one person, i.e. an audit team, then the auditor becomes the team leader and will be responsible for briefing the team and controlling the audit. The individuals selected as audit team members need not be from the quality assurance function. They should, however, have undergone training and indoctrination in auditing techniques and should not have direct responsibility for any of the work in the areas to be audited.

(2) Notify the auditee
This should be done in writing with at least seven days notice of the intention to conduct an audit. Initially, the auditor (or team leader in the case of major audits) should informally contact the auditee to confirm the scheduled date and to discuss the audit scope and timetable, but confirmation of all such discussions should be made formally. In the case of internal audits, the notification would normally be in the form of an internal memo and should include, as a minimum, the following information:

— date and time of audit,
— audit scope and objectives,
— name(s) of auditor(s),
— request to advise if date and time should not be convenient.

An example of a typical notification memo is given as Fig. 7.3.

Externally the formal notification would be much more detailed and should include, as a minimum, the following information:

INTER-OFFICE MEMORANDUM

TO: S. J. BRYAN — PLANNING DEPARTMENT
FROM: N. DOE — QUALITY ASSURANCE
SUBJECT: DEPARTMENT AUDIT   **DATE**: 23 JULY 1990

This is to confirm the arrangements for the forthcoming scheduled audit of your department's quality system.

        Date of audit: 30 July 1990
        Time of audit: commencing 1000 hours

The audit scope and objectives are to verify the implementation and effectiveness of the following procedural documents:

— procedure XYZ-PLA-001 rev.2 Contract review meetings
— procedure XYZ-PLA-002 rev.1 Progress reporting.

The audit team will consist of N. Doe (team leader) and J. Jones.

Please contact the undersigned should these arrangements not be convenient.

Regards,

N. Doe
Audit team leader

Fig. 7.3 — Typical internal audit notification memo.

— date and time of audit,
— audit scope and objectives,
— name(s) of auditor(s),
— audit timetable or itinerary,
— invitation to senior management to attend both entry and exit meetings,
— request for escorts to be available to accompany each member of the audit team,
— request for office and other facilities to be made available,
— request to confirm the arrangements (RSVP).

An example of a typical external notification letter is given as Fig. 7.4.

    Having made the formal notification, then all relevant information relating to the activities or functions to be audited should be obtained.

Stebbing and Partners INTERNATIONAL

QUALITY MANAGEMENT CONSULTANTS

Mr. A.N. Other   9 July 1990
Quality Manager
The XYZ Services Company Limited
Acme House
First Street
Primaton

Dear Mr Other,

Quality Assurance Audit Notification

This letter is to confirm our intention to undertake a quality
audit of The XYZ Services Company Limited on Monday and Tuesday
the 30 and 31 July 1990. The purpose of the audit is to verify
compliance with the requirements of your quality manual and, in
particular, your procedures for the control of: documentation;
purchasing; internal audit and corrective action.

Our audit team will comprise Mr. L. E. Stebbing (team leader),
Mr. B. Woodhouse and Mr. J.L. Jones.

The audit will commence with the entry meeting at 0930 on 30
July 1990 and will be followed by the audit review, which is
scheduled to commence at 1000 and to continue through until 1630
with a break for lunch and will recommence at 0930 on the 31
July, continuing through until 12 noon. The exit meeting is
provisionally scheduled to commence at 1430 on 31 July.

It would be appreciated if you could arrange for representatives
of your senior management to be available to attend both the
entry and exit meetings.

It is our intention that the audit should be conducted with the
minimum of disruption to your normal work programme. It would
be appreciated, therefore, if you could arrange also for the
provision of office facilities for our audit team and for the
necessary cognizant personnel to be available to accompany each
member of the team during the audit.

Would you please confirm that these arrangements are acceptable.
Should you have any queries with regard to this forthcoming audit
please do not hesitate to contact the undersigned.

Yours sincerely,

N.DOE, Quality Manager

Fig. 7.4 — External audit notification letter.

(3) Agree the audit timetable
This should be done in conjunction with the auditee. The timetable should be planned to be most effective and to avoid involving too many people. It is considered good practice to plan to commence audit proceedings at least half an hour after the auditee's commencement of work. This gives time for the auditee to prepare for the day's work and to allocate responsibilities to those not involved in the audit.

A late finish should be avoided where possible as the auditee could have other pressing matters to attend to, the concern for which may make the auditee less attentive to the audit.

(4) Identify, obtain and review all relevant documentation
This refers to documents such as procedures, job instructions, process verification plans, specifications, and others. If a previous audit has already been carried out, then the report of that audit should form part of this documentation. There may be corrective actions still outstanding, which should be followed up. Once all relevant information has been reviewed the next step should be taken.

(5) Brief audit team members
The audit team leader would be accountable for briefing the team members as to their responsibilities within the audit. The team leader assumes total charge of the audit and must ensure that all team members are aware of the part they must play. At this juncture he/she would allocate audit tasks to the team members based upon their areas of expertise and would assign to them the appropriate documentation. Each team member should then review the documentation and develop their own check-lists.

(6) Develop an audit check-list
A check-list is not a mandatory exercise but it is strongly recommended. In developing a check-list, the auditor would be required to read all the relevant documents in depth. This should then make the auditor familiar with the auditee's activities, which would lead to a greater understanding between the two parties. A check-list also acts as an *aide-memoire* and governs the continuity and depth of the audit.

Many organizations utilize standard pre-prepared check-lists but the use of these generally results in the audit becoming a mechanical exercise on the part of the auditor, with the auditee becoming little more than an answering machine. Such audits became merely routine and may be of little value. Every audit should, to a certain extent, be a one-off.

Check-lists should be developed utilizing the system or procedural criteria. The procedural documents, if established to an agreed format, should be auditable documents and would readily lend themselves to check-list development.

An example of a typical check-list is given as Fig. 7.5.

		QUALITY MANAGEMENT SYSTEMS		Page of
Stebbing and Partners INTERNATIONAL		ASSESSMENT/AUDIT CHECK LIST		
ITEM No.	REQUIREMENT	ACTIVITY COMPLIANCE	COMMENTS/REMARKS	

Form Q0083

Fig. 7.5 — Audit check-list.

When developing check-lists for the audit of procedural activities (the adherence or compliance audit) care should be taken not to include items which would not produce objective evidence. The procedure for auditing should give the auditor the flexibility to determine whether an activity is acceptable or not, rather than a strict YES or NO. There are some instances where an activity may not be strictly in accordance with procedure but may otherwise be perfectly acceptable. It is, therefore, prudent to denote acceptability and qualify the result.

PERFORMANCE OF THE AUDIT

Again, as for the preparation and planning phase, the performance phase is subdivided into a number of distinct activities. There are four in all but these should not be confused with the four phases of the total audit process. They are:

(1) The entry meeting.
(2) The audit itself.
(3) Evaluation of results.
(4) The exit meeting.

(1) The entry meeting

Upon arrival at the audit venue, the auditor (or audit team leader) should convene a brief meeting between the auditor and the auditee. This meeting is given many titles such as entry meeting, entry interview, pre-audit meeting, opening meeting and others.

The purpose of an entry meeting is to:

— introduce the auditor (or audit team) to the representatives of the auditee, if they are not already known to each other;
— confirm briefly the purpose and scope of the audit;
— review the audit scope, timetable and agenda;
— provide a short summary of the methods and procedures to be used to conduct the audit;
— clarify any ambiguities of the audit process;
— introduce the method by which any non-conformances will be addressed (i.e. the corrective action request);
— agree a tentative time for the closing meeting and invite senior management of the auditee to attend;
— arrange for escorts to accompany the audit team;
— in the case of external audits, confirm that suitable office facilities and resources will be made available to the audit team;
— and, also in the case of external audits, arrange to undertake a familiarization tour of the facility, if time permits.

The names of those present should be recorded. An attendance register (Fig. 7.6) is a suitable document for this. It should be stressed, however, that names and positions should be printed to retain legibility. The author is in great favour of utilizing the attendance register both for internal and external activities as not everyone has business cards and the correct spelling of a person's name is very important.

(2) The audit itself

This should be conducted using the prepared check-lists as a guide. These check-lists could be expanded, if necessary, to determine compliance with specified requirements and/or determine the effectiveness of the implementation of a system's element.

Objective evidence should be collected and examined and details recorded on the check-list. All essential information, for example, identification of the evidence examined, specific details of non-conforming or adverse

ATTENDANCE REGISTER	
SUBJECT:	
DATE:	
NAME	TITLE/ORGANIZATION

Form Q0085

Fig. 7.6 — Attendance register.

conditions, together with any applicable references, should also be recorded. If they appear significant, any clues suggesting a non-conformance should be noted and investigated, though they may not have been covered by the check-list. Information gained by interviews should be corroborated by acquiring the same information from other independent sources.

In completing the audit check-list under the heading '**Activity compliance**' the auditor should state 'acceptable', 'not acceptable', 'not applicable' (N/A) or 'see comment'. The '**Comments/remarks**' column should be used to expand on the activity or to reference objective evidence and non-conformances.

When a non-conformance is identified, it is good practice to request the auditee to acknowledge the finding by appending his/her signature, or initials, to the objective evidence documented in the check-list. It should be explained that such an acknowledgement does not mean that a request for corrective action will be issued. This will be decided when the results of the total audit are subsequently evaluated.

During the audit, in order to ensure the optimal achievement of audit objectives, it may become necessary to make changes to the auditors' work assignments and perhaps to the audit itinerary or timetable. This is the responsibility of the team leader and any such changes should be made in agreement with the auditee. Should the audit objectives appear to become unattainable, then the team leader should make the decision to abort the audit and should report the reasons to the auditee and to his/her own management.

(3) Evaluation of results

Upon completion of the audit, and before the closing meeting, the audit team should meet to consider and evaluate the evidence generated during the audit. The team should analyse any apparent non-conformances or adverse conditions to ensure validity as audit findings. This analysis should also take place even when only a single auditor is concerned. Objective evidence of a departure from approved procedures, documented requirements and/or other applicable documents should be considered as valid justification for an audit finding. Such audit findings should be recorded and a document known as a corrective action request (CAR) form is a typical vehicle for this. An example is given in Fig. 7.7.

The CAR form should be completed by the auditor to show only the nature of the non-conformance. The sections for 'Corrective action', 'Action taken to prevent recurrence' of a non-conformance and 'Follow-up and Close-out' should be left blank at this stage.

Having reviewed the audit findings and completed any necessary CAR forms, the auditor (or audit team leader) should convene a meeting with the auditee to discuss the outcome of the audit. This meeting, like the entry meeting, is given many titles, such as closing meeting, exit meeting, exit interview, post-audit meeting, and others.

(4) The exit meeting

At this meeting should be present the auditee and, as necessary, management representatives. The names of all persons attending the meeting should again be recorded in the same manner as for the entry meeting.

QUALITY MANAGEMENT SYSTEMS	CAR No.

Stebbing and Partners INTERNATIONAL	CORRECTIVE ACTION REQUEST	DATE AUDIT No.

COMPANY/DEPARTMENT AUDITED & ADDRESS

BASIS OF AUDIT:

AUDITOR	COMPANY/DEPT. REPRESENTATIVE	AREA AUDITED

NON-CONFORMANCE

SIGNED* .... SIGNED ....
    COMPANY/DEPT. REPRESENTATIVE   AUDITOR
* Signature indicates understanding not concurrence

CORRECTIVE ACTION

DATE CORRECTIVE ACTION TO BE COMPLETED

SIGNED .... DATE:
COMPANY/DEPT. REPRESENTATIVE

ACTION TAKEN TO PREVENT RECURRENCE

DATE ACTION TO PREVENT RECURRENCE TO BE COMPLETED:

SIGNED ...., DATE:
COMPANY/DEPT. REPRESENTATIVE

FOLLOW-UP AND CLOSE OUT
PROPOSED FOLLOW-UP DATE:
FOLLOW-UP DETAILS

DATE CAR CLOSED: SIGNED ....
                                                AUDITOR

Form Q0092

Fig. 7.7 — Corrective action request.

During this meeting, the auditor (or team leader) should present an overview of the audit results and should present any findings and ensure that such findings are understood by the auditee. At this stage the CARs (if any) should be presented to the auditee and the auditee requested to sign the first section of the form to indicate an understanding of the non-conformance. The signature does not indicate an agreement, only an acknowledgement that the finding is understood. A copy of each CAR is left with the auditee. The auditor (or team leader) should emphasize at this stage that it has not been possible to cover every aspect of the auditee's quality system. It does not follow, therefore, that where no non-conformances have been reported none exist.

The auditor (or team leader) should advise the auditee of the intended issue date of the formal audit report. Generally this should be within ten working days from the date of the exit meeting. It is standard practice to attach the originals of the CARs to the audit report and the auditor (or team leader) should make this clear.

The auditee should be requested to respond to the findings, usually within ten working days of the receipt of the audit report. This response entails the auditee returning the originals of the CARs to the auditing function, indicating on the form:

— the corrective action which is to be taken to correct the deficiency, the date by which this will be done and signing it in the appropriate place;
— the corrective action which is to be taken to prevent a recurrence of the deficiency, the date by which this will be done and also signing it in the appropriate place.

It is to be stressed that the response due date is not the date by which the corrective action, and action to prevent recurrence, is expected to be completed but the date by which the CAR is to be returned.

Having presented the audit results to senior management and clarified any ambiguities, the audit team should then withdraw. It is not unusual for an auditee to request the auditor to make recommendations to correct the deficiencies. Internally this could be expected of the auditor but nevertheless it should be made clear that any recommendations made are purely personal and should not be taken as an instruction.

Externally extreme caution must be taken when making recommendations, as the auditor may be taken to account if such recommendations are subsequently found to be ineffective. It is up to the auditee to determine the extent and the methods for corrective and subsequent preventative actions.

At the exit meeting, the auditee may produce objective evidence which may nullify a corrective action. Any such evidence should be evaluated to confirm that not only does it correct the deficiency but it also prevents a recurrence of the deficiency. Should it satisfy both counts, then the CAR should not be withdrawn but closed-out (completed) in the normal way with a copy being left with the auditee and recorded accordingly in the audit report.

There may be instances also where the auditee declines to acknowledge a finding on the CAR, in which case the team leader would indicate on the CAR that the auditee declined to sign. This would be recorded in the audit report.

THE AUDIT REPORT

The audit report should be prepared by, or under the direction of, the audit team leader who should be responsible for its accuracy and completeness.

The report should contain the following information, as applicable:

— organization audited (company, department, function);
— scope and objectives of the audit;
— details of the audit itinerary or timetable;
— identification of the audit team members;
— identification of auditee's representatives;
— identification of the audit criteria (quality system standard, quality manual, procedures, job instructions, contract workscope, and others);
— record of non-conformances;
— the result of the audit;
— audit report distribution list.

Audit reports, as for any other series of documents, should be presented in a uniform manner and the formulation of such covered by procedure. A typical audit report would comprise the following:

— lead (or cover) sheet (Fig. 7.8),
— report sheet (Fig. 7.9),
— CARs,
— covering letter.

If so required the completed check-lists could be included as part of the audit report. This practice, however, is not recommended as it adds to the amount of paper distributed and could lead to disagreements with the auditee regarding the objective evidence listed. The completed check-lists should be filed with a copy of the audit report.

The results of the audit should be summarized on the lead sheet and any audit findings (CARs) should be itemized. By giving a summary on the first page management is enabled to see at a glance the outcome of the audit. If

	QUALITY MANAGEMENT SYSTEMS	AUDIT REPORT No.
Stebbing and Partners INTERNATIONAL	AUDIT REPORT	Page 1 of

CONTRACT: CONTRACT No.

AUDITED ORGANISATION   PURCHASE ORDER No.

ADDRESS   AUDIT CRITERIA

                                         DATE OF AUDIT

TEL. No,   DATE PREVIOUS AUDIT

PERSONS CONTACTED   PREVIOUS AUDIT No.

                                         AUDIT TEAM

SUMMARY OF AUDIT

SIGNED ....   SIGNED ....,.......
          (TEAM LEADER)   (PROJECT QUALITY ASSURANCE MANAGER)

DATE   DATE

Form Q0086

Fig. 7.8 — Audit report — lead (or cover) sheet.

	QUALITY MANAGEMENT SYSTEMS	AUDIT REPORT No.
Stebbing and Partners INTERNATIONAL	AUDIT REPORT	Page of

Form Q0087

Fig. 7.9 — Audit report sheet.

further information is required, then reference can be made to the details in the body of the report.

An audit summary could read as follows:

Summary of audit

> The purpose of this audit was to verify the implementation of document control as covered by procedure No. ... (here state document number, title and revision status). The audit indicated that generally the requirements of the procedure were being implemented but there were certain areas which would appear to require much closer attention.
>
> Deficiencies were identified with regard to the delegation of responsibility, the control of document distribution, the review of documentation and maintaining records up to date. These deficiencies have been addressed by a total of six corrective action requests Nos. 001–006 inclusive.

The body of the report should follow a prescribed format and, as an example, should report on:

— the entry meeting,
— the audit itself,
— the exit meeting,
— follow-up,
— general observations.

Each heading, if this format is used, should always appear in the report and when a heading is not applicable the words 'not applicable' should follow beneath the heading. To explain this more fully:

Entry meeting

Provide a brief summary of the meeting, stating who attended; alternatively attach a copy of the attendance register to the report. Avoid too much detail; entry meetings usually follow a very standard pattern. List any specific requests made and/or agreements reached with the auditee.

Audit

Give a detailed account of the audit, listing the areas which were found to be satisfactory and in compliance with requirements. Detail the areas which were not in compliance with requirements and which it was necessary to address by CARs. Include as 'observations of concern' activities which were deficient but which were not addressed by CARs. If considered appropriate, make constructive 'recommendations' to the auditee for rectifying the deficiency but do not be dogmatic (auditees will usually find another way of correcting a deficiency in any case).

Exit meeting

Provide a brief summary of the meeting, stating who attended (as for entry meetings, avoid too much detail). Exit meetings usually follow a standard pattern. Record if any CARs are closed out as a result of further discussion and additional information being provided at the exit meeting. Record if the auditee declined to sign a CAR (this will also be stated on the CAR form by the audit team leader).

Follow-up

If the audit included any follow-up activity from a previous audit this could be stated here and the results detailed. State the intention to undertake a follow-up audit to verify close-out of each CAR, usually within a defined period of the final date stated for the completion of corrective action and the action to prevent a recurrence of the identified deficiencies.

General observations

Include any general observations considered applicable and constructive. As an example:

> Although generally the requirements of the procedures were being implemented, more attention is required adequately to control document distribution, documentation review and the maintenance of up-to-date records.

If there are no 'general observations' add 'not applicable' beneath this heading.

When complete, the audit report should then be signed on the cover sheet by the auditor (or audit team leader) and by the appropriate supervisor (corporate quality assurance manager, senior manager, etc.) after he/she has reviewed the report and the contents have his/her approval.

The original of any CAR raised as a result of the audit should accompany the audit report when it is forwarded to the auditee.

It is considered good practice to ensure that the audit report is completed and issued to the auditee, under a covering memo, within fourteen days (ten working days) of the final date of the audit. The covering letter should indicate the final date by which responses are required for the audit findings/CARs.

Report distribution
It is usual to present the report to senior management of the auditee, any additional distribution being determined in accordance with company policy or, in the case of external audits, in consultation with the auditee at the exit meeting. In the case of external audits, audit reports containing confidential or proprietary information should be suitably safeguarded by the auditing organization.

Report and record retention
Audit documents should be retained in accordance with company policy or again, in the case of external audits, by agreement reached between the auditing organization and the auditee. Regulatory requirements should also be taken into consideration when determining record retention periods.

THE FOLLOW-UP

The auditee is responsible for determining and initiating the corrective action necessary to correct a deficiency and to correct the cause of the deficiency. The auditor should be responsible only for identifying the deficiency.

Corrective and preventative actions should be completed within a time-scale determined by the auditee but which is acceptable to the auditing organization. Subsequent follow-up actions should also be similarly undertaken to an agreed time-scale.

Following receipt of the responses to the audit findings, the auditor (or audit team leader) should initiate follow-up activities, usually in the form of another audit, to verify the completion of the action to correct the deficiency and the action taken to prevent recurrence.

If the follow-up indicates that the actions taken have corrected and prevented a recurrence of the deficiency, then the CAR can be closed-out. This should be stated on the CAR form in the appropriate section.

If the follow-up indicates that the action taken does not correct the deficiency or does not prevent a recurrence, then this should be stated on the CAR form in the 'follow-up' section of the form and the deficiency readdressed by issuing a new CAR.

It may be necessary, in the event of a continuing deficiency, for the auditor to call in support from senior management — hence the requirement of all quality system standards that the quality assurance function reports direct to senior management. Audits, audit reports, CARs and follow-up audits should be controlled and regulated. It is, therefore, prudent to establish and maintain details of all such activities.

Fig. 7.10 is a typical example of an audit report status log, while Fig. 7.11 shows a typical example of a CAR status log.

Traceability of documentation is, once again, most important. It will be

AUDIT REPORT STATUS LOG								
AUDIT REPORT No:	AUDIT TYPE	AUDIT TEAM LEADER	AUDIT DATE	COMPANY/ DEPARTMENT/ DISCIPLINE AUDITED	PROCEDURES/ CRITERIA AUDITED	CONTRACT/ PURCHASE ORDER No:	DATE AUDIT REPORT ISSUED	CAR's ISSUED

Form Q0082

Fig. 7.10 — Audit report status log.

CAR SERIAL No.	CAR ISSUED To	DEFICIENCY	AUDIT DATE	INITIALS OF AUDITOR	RESPONSE DUE DATE	DATE REMINDER SENT	CORRECTIVE ACTION COMPLETION DATE	ACTION PREVENT RECURRENCE COMPLETION DATE	PROPOSED FOLLOW-UP DATE	DATE CAR CLOSED

CORRECTIVE ACTION REQUEST (CAR) STATUS LOG

Form Q0091

Fig. 7.11 — Corrective action request status log.

necessary, therefore, to develop an identification system to control audit reports and CARs. Provision is made for this in the respective status logs.

A typical identification system for internal audits could be a sequence which links the audit to the year during which it was carried out. In the following example the first two numbers represent the year followed by the audit number:

9001, 9002, 9003

and so on. For external applications, a supplier identification, purchase order number or contract number, could be used as a prefix followed by the sequential audit number.

Any CARs issued during an audit should be cross-referenced to the audit itself to retain traceability. The audit number should be used as a prefix followed by the CAR number, which would commence at 1 (one) for every audit. For example, during audit 9001 three CARs may have been issued and would be identified as follows:

9001-01,   9001-02,   9001-03.

THE AUDIT ROUTE

The complete auditing function has been set out in Fig. 7.12 in the form of a flow chart, which takes each activity step by step from the formulation of the quality system through to implementation and adherence. Each activity is identified with the appropriate responsible department and, where applicable, with the interfacing department.

Following the chart through from the establishment of the quality system (a management responsibility), the procedures and instructions are developed and implemented by the appropriate departments. These procedures and instructions are then audited by the quality assurance function to confirm implementation and effectiveness. If compliant and effective, then the audit report is issued to confirm this. If non-compliant or ineffective then, together with an audit report, CARs should be issued on the department concerned. The department should then determine and implement corrective action and the action to prevent recurrence.

If the discrepancy had been a straightforward operator fault, then the action to correct the deficiency would follow the left-hand route on the flow chart. The follow-up audit would either confirm that the action taken to correct the deficiency and to prevent recurrence was satisfactory, in which case the CAR would be closed-out, or the action taken was ineffective, in which case the CAR would be reissued.

The discrepancy may be due to a procedural fault. The activity may have

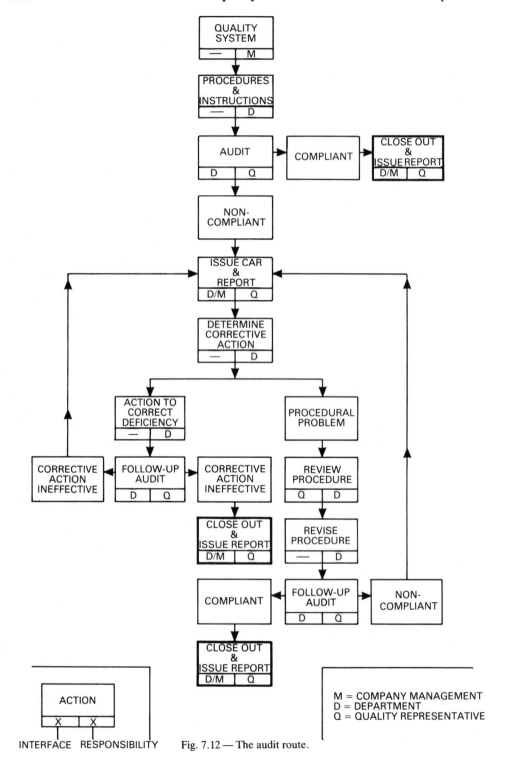

Fig. 7.12 — The audit route.

been incorrectly documented, the activity itself being perfectly effective (this often occurs when procedures are written by personnel other than those who are familiar with the activity). In such a case, an amendment to the procedure would be required. The revision would then be approved, issued and implemented. A follow-up audit would be carried out to confirm implementation and effectiveness, in which case the CAR would be closed-out or, if still non-compliant or ineffective, then the CAR would be reissued. Corrective action could go either way, depending on whether the procedure was still ineffective or whether the operator was at fault, thus completing the loop until eventual satisfactory implementation and close-out. In the event of a continuous non-conformance, it will be necessary to refer the problem to senior management for resolution.

THE AUDITOR — GUIDE, PHILOSOPHER AND FRIEND

Throughout the audit activity, particularly in the early stages of the implementation of quality systems, there are bound to be audit findings. Personnel may well have to get used to doing things differently and the new methods may be foreign to them. The auditor should not adopt a belligerent attitude but should be the guide, philosopher and friend. To adopt the so-called 'gotcher' mentality will lead only to antagonism and non-co-operation.

As has been stated, should a deficiency be found and the auditor asked to make a recommendation regarding corrective action, then he can by all means assist in this respect but it is prudent for the auditor to advise the auditee that the advice given is purely personal and should not be taken as 'gospel'. Wherever possible the auditee should be left to determine his/her own corrective action.

Experience has shown that recommending corrective action (particularly in the case of external audits) can create more problems than it solves. The recommended corrective action is invariably taken as an instruction and, when the recommendation is found to be ineffective, the auditor usually finds the blame laid at his door.

Corrective action, where a major deficiency is concerned, may involve the auditee in a great deal of time and money. In such instances should the auditee act upon a recommendation which is ineffective in its result, then the auditee could well be inclined to submit an invoice for the costs involved.

An auditor should be aware of the implications when recommending corrective action and, therefore, should be very sure of his/her ground. One must have experience with the activity under audit. In many instances, particularly where auditors are inexperienced, the recommendation made when a non-compliant action is discovered is to amend the procedure. Amending the procedure is an easy let-out. A follow-up audit by an experienced auditor usually uncovers the truth. The auditee had not read the procedure in the first place and was, therefore, not aware of the requirement. It is a management responsibility to make all personnel aware of their commitments.

Once a deficiency has been discovered and reported upon, it is worthwhile keeping in touch with the auditee to evaluate the progress of corrective action. This acts as a spur to the auditee and reminds him/her of their responsibilities. It could also highlight any problems which the auditee may be experiencing with regard to close-out.

As well as being a guide, philosopher and friend, the auditor should also have many other attributes.

AUDITOR QUALIFICATION AND TRAINING

The audit has set out to examine the adequacy of the system for assuring quality. As for the financial audit, one would expect the auditor to be qualified and experienced. A quality audit is not as simple as it may appear and the auditor must have the right background and personality to undertake the audit. The auditor requires, apart from the appropriate competence in the field in which he/she is working, a knowledge of:

— quality management principles and practices,
— quality practices of the industry concerned,
— planning,
— auditing techniques.

In conclusion, the results of countless audits undertaken by the author indicate, and continue to indicate, that generally the major problem areas encountered by most companies are caused by:

— insufficient planning,
— insufficient training,
— inadequate control of documentation,
— the absence of a system for internal quality audits,
— inadequate control over purchasing activities.

As will be seen, the above five problem areas constitute fifty per cent of the *ten essential elements*, which must indicate the need for a well-controlled and implemented quality management system.

Once the initial quality management objectives of the company have been achieved and found to be working effectively and efficiently, with all personnel appreciating the benefits of such a system, the time is then ripe to introduce quality improvement techniques. The introduction of quality circles is one such technique which we shall now consider.

8

Quality circles and problem solving techniques

No question is ever settled, until it is settled right.
Ella Wheeler Wilcox (1855–1919), *Settle the question right.*

Quality circles can play a very important role within a quality management system but it is to be emphasized that circles are a part and only a part of the total quality concept. Circles should not be considered an end in themselves but more in the nature of a means to an end.

Many organizations believe, or have been led to believe, that by implementing quality circles all quality problems would be solved. Naturally, such organizations become very disillusioned when it is discovered that such is not the case. Despite this warning, however, quality circles are one aspect of quality management most likely to be adopted by the service industry who might find the more formalized approach in the rest of this book 'too difficult' whereas a 'circle programme' would appear to be deceptively easy to arrange.

Circles are a method of organizing employee participation in the improvement of a process, the process itself being any activity undertaken by any section of the workforce, even though no tangible product may be produced. As has been said, the internal product is the result of one's own endeavours and thus everyone concerned in any given process should be given the opportunity to contribute his or her knowledge and experience in a team effort to improve process capability and thus increase job satisfaction.

WHAT ARE QUALITY CIRCLES?

Quality circles are groups of four to twelve people who perform similar roles and who generally come from the same work area. The author is of the opinion, however, that circles can be more effective if some members have dissimilar roles and could bring a fresh mind to bear on discussions and, although the exercise should be voluntary, people might be asked (not directed) to join, so as to ensure an interchange of ideas. These people meet on a regular basis to identify and analyse problems and to establish solutions to the problems. The solutions are then presented to management for evaluation and approval. The circle is then often responsible for implementation and effectiveness of the solution.

The quality circle operates in a similar fashion to the quality assurance auditor, whereby a deficiency (problem) is identified, corrective action is taken to correct the deficiency and action taken to prevent recurrence. As for any form of corrective action, there must be management involvement if action is to be effective.

Quality circles relate directly to the quality of the item and/or service and, as with any verification exercise, there is no direct involvement in activities which occurred previously. What is more, a single quality circle would deal only with problems or subjects related specifically to its own area of operation, although some solutions may affect other work areas.

It has been widely assumed, quite wrongly, that quality circles will work only in a manufacturing environment. Any organization, where numbers of people are engaged in similar activities, can utilize circle techniques. Indeed, many financial and business organizations have successfully implemented circles as part of their overall quality strategy. Neither should it be assumed that quality circles are formed to discuss only process-related problems.

As the circle members will be experts in their own particular function, their knowledge and experience should be utilized to suggest ways of increasing job satisfaction, which should, in turn, enhance the quality of their working life.

The Japanese are considered to be experts in quality circle applications and, because of their success in this direction, many Western organizations are led to believe that circles are a Japanese invention. This is not entirely the case. Circles certainly developed in Japan following the introduction, from the USA, of statistical quality control methods during the 1950s. The Japanese success has received international acclaim and Western industries are now looking towards achieving similar successes. The author, having worked in Japan for many years, has been able to understand, to a certain extent, the Japanese way of thinking and consequently is convinced that, because of the wide differences between Western and Japanese culture, the West may not achieve the same success in circle implementation. This, however, should not deter Western organizations from adopting circle philosophies, as indeed any success, however small, must be considered worthwhile, providing implementation costs do not exceed the beneficial results.

THE COMPANY-WIDE APPROACH

Any philosophy which enhances the quality of the service or product should be implemented on a company-wide basis. Quality circles could be considered as one of the tools in the total quality management tool box and, as with any tool, one should acquire the knowledge to use it properly. Such learning would, therefore, require direction. This direction must come from senior management and, as has been said many times before, the commitment must come also from senior management. However, commitment is one thing, support is another! Adequate resources in the way of money, time and people must be made available.

FIRST CONSIDERATIONS

Before embarking on a circle programme, therefore, a number of things should be taken into consideration, such as:

— reasons for introducing a quality circle programme;
— associated costs;
— methods of establishing the circles programme;
— education of management and the work-force in the understanding of, and the benefits and improvements to be derived from, such a programme;
— employee acceptance;
— training;
— organizational structure for circles;
— implementation;
— methods of evaluating effectiveness.

Take each of these in turn.

Reasons for introducing a quality circle programme

An organization should understand that a quality circle programme can produce effective results but it should not be treated as an end to quality problems. Circles are an improvement technique and will not have the desired result without an efficient quality management system in place to deal with the results. The programme should be considered as company-wide and not just an isolated technique which can be switched off and on as effectiveness rises or falls.

Quality circles are introduced for many reasons and the most generally accepted are for improvements in:

— the quality of the product or service,
— employee satisfaction,
— communication,
— employee effectiveness,
— company competitiveness.

It is, therefore, up to each individual organization to establish firmly the reasons before implementing the programme and the reasoning should be made known to the work-force if quality circles are to achieve any success at all. It is, therefore, extremely important that the work-force, together with union representatives, are consulted before any action is taken. The reasons 'why' are important, as has already been established.

Associated costs

Circles are voluntary participation activities but members usually meet in company-paid time. Salaries and wages should, therefore, be taken into account.

It may be considered necessary to employ a consultant to assist in, or even undertake, the development of the circle programme, in which, case consultancy fees must be considered and accounted for.

Costs associated with training of personnel in the application of circles, together with training materials, can be substantial. In some instances, the role of the circles' facilitator, whose responsibilities are described later, could be a full-time occupation.

All these costs should be weighed against the expected benefits and savings.

Methods of establishing the circles programme

The methods adopted when developing and implementing a quality management system are, in many instances, equally applicable when developing and implementing a quality circles programme.

A steering committee, or working party, should be established and the responsibility for the formation of this should lie with a senior member of staff who has knowledge of the activities or processes which are considered to be the most likely to receive the most benefit from the introduction of circles. This person is normally given the title 'facilitator'. In general, facilitators can come from any area but experience has shown that, particularly in a manufacturing environment, most come from one of three areas: production departments, training departments or quality control departments. In service companies such appointments are made based upon the person's understanding of the business and leadership capabilities.

It stands to reason that whoever is appointed to the facilitator position should be totally committed to circle philosophies if the programme is to have any success. It is an important position and that person could well have similar attributes to that of the quality manager and, indeed, there is a very good argument for such an appointment to be made from within the quality management group (providing, of course, the organization concerned is operating to the quality management philosophies put forward in this book).

In addition to the facilitator, the steering committee should include representatives of management, the quality management function, trade unions and/or other employee representatives.

A circle leader is usually chosen from the supervisory staff to whom, in normal everyday circumstances, the circle members would report. This, however, does not preclude others from the responsibility, providing there is evidence of suitable training and experience to support such an appointment.

The steering committee, once established, would then:

(1) determine the requirements for third party (consultancy) assistance in developing the programme, training the participants and the eventual implementation of the scheme;
(2) define responsibilities and lines of communication between individual circles through to management;
(3) communicate to all employees the reasons for, and the benefits to be derived from, the implementation of quality circles.

Education of the work-force
It is recommended that this be carried out by third-party sources — a consultant. Again, experience has shown that, by utilizing the capabilities of someone outside the organization, much more credence is given to the subject. The utilization of third-party sources leads to a much greater employee acceptance (the prophet from another country).

Training
Quality circles will never be effective if the work-force is just formed into a collection of departmental or functional groups and told to get on with it. Training in many areas should be given and these areas would include:

— methods of data collection,
— problem solving techniques,
— leadership skills,

— brainstorming sessions,
— presentation techniques.

Once a problem has been identified then, of course, the techniques of collecting the data and solving the problems do not come automatically — they should be taught.

The skills of leadership, as for management, do require training and experience.

Brainstorming sessions have been found invaluable in problem solving but the leader of the session should have had the necessary training to evaluate the results effectively.

Presentation techniques are fundamental to quality circles. The circle leader and his team should have the ability to put forward to management, both orally and by means of visual aids, what the problem is, how it was identified and the suggested methods of solving the problem. The suggested methods must be supported by evidence and by proper costing to substantiate the recommendation. A solution to a problem could go unheeded because of inadequate preparation and poor presentation.

In general, most facilitators receive training from third-party sources. The facilitators, in turn, are normally responsible for circle leader training, with the circle members then receiving training from the facilitator, the circle leader or a combination of both.

Some data collection and problem solving techniques, as outlined above, will be discussed later in this chapter.

Organizational structure for circles
The organizational structure for quality circles has already been touched upon but it is worthwhile looking at in a little more detail.

As has already been said, quality circles are voluntary participation activities — they are for the members. It is well-known that, in most organizations where there are successful circle programmes, the circle members become so identified with their respective circles that they give their circle a club atmosphere by giving it a name such as 'The Cubs', 'The Inner Circle', 'The Family Circle' and so on. One particular circle, operating in the manufacturing sector of industry, whose members worked in very hot and humid conditions, was named 'The Devil's Disciples' — rather apt, and a very efficient circle which was instrumental in improving working conditions as well as product quality.

The circle's objectives are to identify problems, develop solutions and then present the complete case to management for consideration with the view to eventual approval and implementation. The philosophy of quality circles has been called 'management from the bottom upwards'.

Management is, in effect, delegating some of its responsibilities to the work-force. This should, therefore, relieve management of some of the mundane but time-consuming and important tasks, thus giving more time to the solving of company policy issues. Another advantage of such a form of delegation is that it leads to a better and more open form of communication, which can, in turn, lead only to an enhancement in employee–management relationships.

The organization should, therefore, start with the circle members themselves. Membership should be strictly voluntary with no enforced membership. Conversely, no one should be banned from membership.

Each circle should appoint a circle leader and it is usual for this leader to be a supervisor in normal everyday circumstances.
Circles, to be effective, should liaise with each other, so that related problems can be discussed. There is, therefore, the need for a co-ordinator — the co-ordinator is the facilitator already referred to. The facilitator provides the link not only between individual circles but also between the circles and management. As such, the facilitator would be instrumental in overseeing the development of the circle programme and assisting with, and co-ordinating, the circle meetings. This person will also watch over circle activities with regard to problem identification and solving and the eventual implementation of solutions. Obtaining the necessary funding for the circle programme will also be within the realm of the facilitator.

In some large organizations where circle programmes are identified for several locations with two or more facilitators, there would be a requirement for an upper structure co-ordinator to bring it all together. A 'senior facilitator' perhaps!
The circle leaders are primarily responsible for the effectiveness of the meetings and should ensure that all circle members are adequately trained in the problem solving techniques which were previously touched upon.

Implementation

Areas or activities which can benefit from quality circle participation are areas where people work together and experience similar problems. Typically these could cover:

Accounts,
Administration,
Sales and marketing,
Customer service — retail (counters and check-outs),
Reception (hotels),
Patient admissions (hospitals),

Patient care,
Passenger check-in (travel),

and there will be other examples.

Each circle within any of these areas should set itself a project. Initially, until circle members are practised in problem solving, the projects should be small in nature. It is a well-known fact that the smaller problems, which can be quickly solved and which are generally overlooked by management, can have a much greater impact upon the well-being of the work-force and the company as a whole than the solutions to major problems which involve considerable expenditure in cost, time and resources and affect only a small part of the business with limited beneficial results.

Some examples of activities for circle consideration are:

— office administration control,
— rectification work,
— maintenance (hotels/hospitals),
— patient records,
— document control,
— invoicing,
— customer liaison,
— customer complaints.

A schedule should be developed for circle meetings. Invariably the type of project chosen will dictate the frequency of meetings. On average these will probably be once a week at a predetermined time. The length of the meeting should be limited and experience has shown that one hour is usually adequate. A well-chaired meeting of one hour can usually achieve far more than a two-hour free-for-all. Hence the need for a well-trained leader; otherwise the circle might degenerate into a time-wasting talking shop.

A systematic approach should be made to problem solving. The causes should be investigated and solutions discussed and tested. Documentary evidence should be developed to support the anticipated effectiveness of the proposed solution.

Circle leaders should consider also whether the project will have an effect on other circles. In such cases, there could be a need to invite the other 'affected' circle's leader to the meeting.

Problems can, in many instances, be solved quicker if experts or specialists are invited. For example, the project under review may relate to patient home care; it would be prudent, therefore, to invite someone from say the medical or occupational therapy department to give some expert advice.

Methods of evaluating effectiveness

The methods of evaluating effectiveness can be many and varied. A lot will depend on the nature of the project.

Production-related problems, which have been 'solved' by circle members, could result in tangible savings in areas such as:

— reduction in scrap
— reduction in repairs/reworking
— speed-up in unit assembly.

In the main, experience has shown that the benefits resulting from the introduction of quality circle programmes are:

— improvements in quality and efficiency
— improvements in communication and co-operation
— improvements in management-employee relationships
— enhanced job satisfaction.

Improvements in quality and efficiency can be measured in monetary terms provided management is aware of quality costs. Improvements in communication and co-operation are difficult to measure in monetary terms but their effect can be seen in the improvements in management-employee relationship. Enhanced job satisfaction should lead to a greater feeling of 'belonging' and should result in a reduction of absenteeism with increased efficiency.

PROBLEM SOLVING

Quality circles, as has been said, are set up to identify and analyse problems and establish solutions to the problems. Identifying a problem is the easiest part of a circle's activity. We are all very good at identifying problems and would be only too anxious to air them, but do we have sufficient information to analyse what causes them?

In order to discuss and evaluate a problem, which can be either service- or product-related, it will be necessary, in the first instance, to collect all the available information pertaining to that problem and, having obtained all the associated data, it will then be possible to analyse these data and to discuss and evaluate methods of disposing of, or reducing the effects of, the problem. Assessment of available data is, therefore, the first stage of the analysis. The second stage is to determine what further data should be collected and how these data should be presented and evaluated.

Brainstorming sessions are an ideal method of obtaining a large number of ideas and always work better than individual thought. These sessions are usually undertaken at a quality circle meeting when a problem associated with that circle's activities is presented for discussion. At these sessions each member of the circle is, in turn, given the opportunity to present his/her ideas of the possible causes of the problem with suggested solutions. A time limit is placed on these contributions — usually one minute. If a member has no contribution to make then that person will 'pass' and the next member will 'take up the baton', so to speak. This part of the brainstorming session should be limited to putting forward individual ideas. It should be an uninhibited session and no other member should interrupt the flow. Members should be encouraged to contribute no matter how 'way-out' the contribution may be. A seemingly idiotic suggestion may well initiate a good one from someone else. The circle leader will list for all to see, usually on a flip-chart or white board, the proffered problem causes and suggested remedies. The session continues until everyone has run out of ideas.

In some instances brainstorming sessions are not completed at the first meeting as the members get a mental block with the number of ideas put forward being very limited. If such is the case, then it is better to postpone the session until the next meeting which will permit the members to 'sleep on it'. This postponement will not only give the members a chance to think further about the subject but also a chance to obtain suggestions from other members of staff.

Once all ideas are exhausted and listed, the circle members will then evaluate the possible causes of the problem under discussion. After full consideration of all possible contributory factors, the circle members then have the task of investigating the most likely cause(s) for the problem's existence.

Once these probable causes have been determined the remedies listed can then be evaluated to decide on the most appropriate solution. Some of the remedies suggested will be obvious and others may border on the trivial but nevertheless all should be considered and evaluated. Most quality problems are due to a combination of causes which can be categorized under the following four headings (known as the 'four M's'): machines, methods, materials and manpower, so the solution may range over the whole area of these 'four M's'.

Under the category of **machines** would be included such items as:

— computers,
— typewriters,
— hospital equipment (which could cover anything from wheelchairs to operating theatre equipment),
— cleaning equipment,

or any type of equipment associated with the business.

Under the category of **methods** would be the procedures or routines associated with carrying out a task.

Under the category of **materials** would be included such things as:

— software,
— stationery,
— drugs,
— cleaning material

and others.

Under the category of **manpower** would of course be the operator skills which would include training requirements.

Perhaps the solution may involve just one of these categories or a combination of them. It may well be that the solution will involve nothing more than a change in a process procedure.

DATA COLLECTION

Having decided on the possible solution to the problem, it will then be necessary to collect all the data associated with the problem area.

Check-lists and defect charts are usually the best means of collecting data but certain decisions must first be made such as:

— whether the data are to be organized around the type of defect, employee, shift, or machine (equipment);
— the period over which the data are to be collected.

The check-sheet should be designed in order that information can be collected with the minimum of effort. It should be borne in mind that the degree of success in solving problems will rely on the value of the information one collects. The most effective method is to break down the activity into a number of sub-activities and to evaluate each accordingly. On the check-list should be recorded the faults, the reasons for rejection and a brief description of the nature of the fault at each sub-activity stage. The faults can then be summated to produce defect data for the entire process.

The information required will have a bearing on where the information can be collected. In the first instance it will be worthwhile examining any records which may be available rather than starting from scratch.

When all the pertinent information is collected it must then be presented into an easily read manner. There are a number of methods of presenting information such as the use of:

— histograms

— pareto diagrams
— scatter diagrams
— cause and effect diagrams (sometimes called fishbone diagrams or Ishikawa diagrams).

The author does not intend to go into detail on these various methods of data presentation as so much valuable information has already been written on the subject by many eminent authors. Suffice to say that a number of publications dealing with the subject of quality circles and problem solving are included in the bibliography.

However, the process does not finish there. Once a solution, or solutions, have been agreed upon the circle must then evaluate the cost of implementing the solution, together with the anticipated savings, and present the findings to management in a convincing manner.

PRESENTING THE SOLUTIONS TO MANAGEMENT

It is an unfortunate fact of quality circle life that many hours can be spent by a circle in evaluating and solving a problem with the results being rejected by management owing to inadequate presentation. The importance of good presentation cannot be overstressed but what should be borne in mind is that the recommendations of a quality circle might be regarded by management as a criticism of management effectiveness — which, in fact, they probably are. It therefore behoves:

(1) The report to be presented with extreme tact and care — being right is not enough!
(2) management to be receptive to new ideas.

The presentation of the results not only gives management the information required to assess the viability of the recommended corrective action but it also assists with other important aspects of circle activity such as the development of communication and leadership skills.

The presentation of results to management is most effective if use is made of visual aids in the form of overhead slides or large diagrams. Such visual aids, however, should not contain wordy information; diagrams, drawings, pictures and charts hold the attention much better than a list of words.

It should also be borne in mind that, in many cases, the circle members themselves are the experts in the activity and know far more about the subject than the audience. If this is realized then the presenter will have the confidence to talk from a position of strength.

It makes a great deal of sense to rehearse the presentation before giving it to management. Try it out on one's colleagues first.

THE STEPS TO EFFECTIVE PRESENTATION

There are a number of steps to effective presentation and these are:

— take time to plan and prepare for the presentation,
— think carefully about the audience,
— tailor the presentation to the type of audience,
— check all equipment and materials before the presentation,
— be positive,
— prepare for awkward questions and negative attitudes,
— put forward the points in a logical order,
— keep the presentation short and to the point,
— use innovative visual aids,
— speak up and slowly,
— avoid jargon which may be unfamiliar to the audience,
— maintain eye contact with the audience,
— be natural but avoid informality,
— distribute any hand-outs after the presentation.

A quality circle programme will not solve all problems. Circles, where implemented, should be only a part of a company's quality management system — an integral part where no activity is subservient to the other. Each activity — administration, sales, marketing, procurement, customer liaison, the service process itself, after sales service, and so on — can benefit from a well-planned and effective circles programme.

9

Management review

He that would know what shall be must consider what hath been.
Scottish proverb, c. 1641.

No system, however effective, will remain current indefinitely. As has been said, internal audits will verify whether or not the systems are adequate and effective, but audits alone will not tell the complete story. There are many other factors which can affect the integrity of the systems and, in the main, these emanate from outside the company. Some examples will be discussed later.

The market orientation of much of the service industry is dynamic. In many instances, instead of working to a specification the work is often directed at satisfying subjective needs of the market. The importance of constant market monitoring is therefore paramount and a company must always be aware of its competition.

Management must have the ability to anticipate change and to be receptive of change. The entire management system should be devised so as to respond rapidly to change as dictated by the market or proposed by internal means, such as quality circles. It is therefore important that a method of reacting rapidly to such changes is incorporated into the quality system.

SCHEDULING OF REVIEWS

Management should, therefore, make a point of scheduling a regular and systematic review and evaluation of the entire quality system. This review is carried out to ensure the continued adequacy and effectiveness of all the elements within the system. The responsibility for undertaking such a review could well lie with the working party, who should meet at appropriate intervals to discuss and evaluate the impact of change as it concerns the company and its quality system.

THE REVIEW PROCEDURE

In order that a management review is carried out in a systematic and effective manner, it will be necessary to develop a documented procedure which should identify the following:

— frequency of reviews,
— initiation of reviews,
— those attending,
— the review itself,
— documentation of results,
— implementation of any changes.

Let us take each in turn.

Frequency of reviews

It should be the responsibility of management to determine how frequently the review of the total system is to be carried out. During the early stages of implementation, reviews are likely to occur quite frequently — say every three months. In the main, these early reviews will tend to concentrate on the results of internal audits. However, as the workforce becomes accustomed to working in a regularly monitored environment, the internal requirements for change decrease. External sources, however, will continue to exert pressure for change and it is these that must be regularly considered. Experience has shown that, in such instances, management reviews should be carried out at least once a year but preferably every six months. There may, of course, be instances where immediate change is required and the review should be initiated on a priority basis.

Initiation of reviews

Management will determine who is to be responsible for calling a review meeting. In many companies this is the quality manager. There may be instances, however, where other members of the management team may consider there is justification in calling for an urgent review. The procedure in such cases should be for the request to be channelled through the quality manager.

Those attending
As has previously been mentioned, the attendees at a management review meeting could well be the working party, with the senior executive as chairman and the quality manager as co-ordinator. It is recommended that all members of the working party attend such reviews, with the addition of any others who may be able to contribute to the discussion.

The review itself
There are a number of items which could be considered at the review. The following list is not meant to be exhaustive:

— results of internal audits,
— customer feedback (complaints),
— results of market research,
— changes in economic situations,
— new or updated legislation,
— new business methods,
— new technology.

Let us take each in turn.

Results of internal audits
There may be instances where audits have indicated a trend towards consistent non-conformances, which may mean a complete management reappraisal in a given area or department. On the other hand, it may well be that audits have shown the system to be continuously effective and that the time is now right to consider quality improvement techniques, such as quality circles, statistical process control, inventory control, and others.

Customer feedback (complaints)
The ability to respond rapidly to customer complaints and to implement corrective action is the hallmark of a well-run company. Customers may also make comment on an aspect of the product or service which could indicate a requirement to amend the some aspect of the service in order to retain a competitive edge. All such feedback should be analysed and acted upon accordingly.

Results of market research
As has been said, a company must keep-up-to date with customer expectations and have the ability to anticipate market changes. It is important, therefore, that the results of constant market monitoring are reviewed regularly.

Changes in economic situations
Fluctuations in currency exchange rates may need to be evaluated to determine impact on the price of the service. Fluctuating interest rates may also have to be considered in a similar light.

New or updated legislation
New legislation may have been issued that applies to the company's activities and which may have an impact on the safety aspects or certification requirements.

New business methods
New business or marketing techniques may have been developed. On occasions, if the company is part of a group, instructions could emanate from group headquarters stipulating new business techniques are to be followed.

New technology
New machinery or equipment may have come on to the market which should be considered as appropriate to the company.

Documentation of results
Whatever the outcome of the review, the results should be documented. Normally, minutes of meetings are quite sufficient provided they are developed to indicate the subject under discussion, the outcome of the discussion and the person(s) responsible for any action which is to be taken.

Documentary evidence should exist to confirm that the review took place, even if the decisions made were to change nothing.

Implementation of any changes
The person, or persons, responsible for implementing any changes should be advised and the appropriate action taken by them. Subsequent internal audits will verify the implementation and effectiveness of such changes.

Fig. 9.1. is a summation of such a review process.

It will be seen that there is no finite end to the application of a quality management system. We have now come full circle and, in the interests of continuous improvement, the entire process of **P–T–A–M–I–R** will have to be repeated:

Plan	what is required to improve the business
Train	personnel in quality improvement techniques
Action	the improvement process
Monitor	the implementation and effectiveness of improvement techniques

Improve   yet again
Review   the entire process.

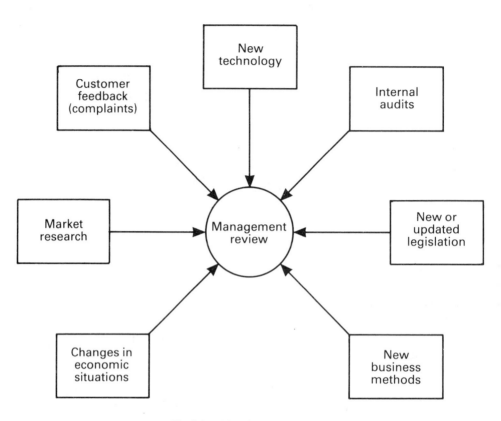

Fig. 9.1 — Management review.

By continually reviewing methods of working and ceaselessly improving the way things are done, the outcome can lead only to enhanced customer satisfaction with the service given, which, in turn, must reflect in increased productivity, efficiency, higher profitability and increased competitiveness.

Appendix A
Typical system element outlines

The elements outlined in this appendix are applicable to all companies regardless of size and product (item or service); the only difference will be in the depth and application of the elements described.

It will be seen that only eight of the ten essential elements are described in this appendix. The **management responsibility** element would be portrayed separately in the policy section of the quality manual. Similarly, **work instructions** would not be described as such, as compliance with this requirement would manifest itself in the documentation of the system.

Function	Outline number
Contract review (Planning)	1
Document control	2
Purchasing	3
Control of non-conforming product	4
Corrective action	5
Quality records	6
Internal quality audits	7
Training	8

The initials XYZ-SCL used in these outlines refer to our fictitious XYZ Services Company Limited.

1   **CONTRACT REVIEW (PLANNING)**

1.1   **General**

1.1.2   Contract review shall apply to either the review of specific customer requirements or to the review and analysis of implied requirements developed as the result of market research.

1.2   **Enquiry documents**

1.2.1   In the case of enquiry documents received from prospective customers these shall be reviewed to ensure that the requirements are understood and all necessary information is available prior to developing the quotation and before its submission to the prospective customer.

1.3   **Contract/research data**

1.3.1   Upon receipt of a contract/order, or upon receipt of market research data, and prior to commencement of any work, provision shall be made by the relevant personnel for a detailed internal review of all relevant information.

1.3.2   This review shall confirm, as applicable, the following criteria:

— work scope,

— customer requirements (stated or implied),

— regulatory requirements,

— relevant national and XYZ-SCL standards and procedures,

1.3.3   As a result of the review, should any of the above items require clarification or amplification, the XYZ-SCL contract manager shall inform the customer and/or research department and maintain an action log until the queries are satisfactorily resolved.

1.3.4   Following the review of contract requirements and/or research data all assigned personnel shall prepare a statement of all criteria for their function prior to commencement of activities. In the case of single person functions, the statement shall be prepared by that person.

1.3.5   Each statement shall contain details of the work scope and lists of the specific applicable customer/data requirements, regulatory requirements and national and XYZ-SCL standards and procedures

1.3.6   The XYZ-SCL contract manager shall ensure the criteria from each function meet the requirements of the contract or research data

1.3.7   It shall be the responsibility of XYZ-SCL management to ensure that all documents referred to in clause 1.3.2 above are maintained up to date by the document control function, with adequate copies to enable them to be accessible to all relevant personnel.

1.3.8   Each function shall maintain a file or have access to each of the referenced documents in clause 1.3.2 above which are applicable to their scope of work.

1.3.9   Details of WHO, WHAT and HOW are defined in XYZ-SCL written procedures and job instructions.

2   **DOCUMENT CONTROL**
2.1   **General**
2.1.1   Provision shall be made adequately to control all documents.
2.1.2   XYZ-SCL shall acknowledge, as applicable, the acceptance of customer imposed requirements and standards which shall be included under the above controls.
2.1.3   The issue, control and recall of all documents shall be under the jurisdiction of the document control manager.
2.1.4   Verification and test plans, and other related instructions, where required by contract, shall be prepared and issued. Activity reports shall be prepared and issued, also as required by contract or as required to meet the company's service schedule.
2.1.5   The system of control shall ensure that all essential documents, contract or data change information, contract instructions, specifications or any other documents are available at the point of use.
2.1.6   Procedures of the latest issue shall be distributed by the document control function to all locations where required for the effective functioning of the quality system.
2.1.7   All documents shall be reviewed and approved for release by the manager of the responsible department in co-ordination with the quality management function.
2.2   **Change to documentation**
2.2.1   All changes to documents shall be implemented in writing and processed in a manner which ensures prompt action at the specified locations. Records shall be maintained of changes as they are made. Documents shall be revised and re-issued, as a new edition, after a practical number of changes have been issued. Written notations on documents shall not be permitted.
2.2.2   A master list shall be established to identify the current revision of documents in order to preclude the use of non-applicable documents.
2.2.3   Provision shall be made to remove and recall all obsolete documents from all points of issue and activity locations.
2.2.4   Requests for changes to customer controlled documents shall be prepared and submitted as prescribed by the customer.
2.3   **Retention of documentation**
2.3.1   When required for traceability purposes a copy of each superseded document, established in accordance with the requirements of the XYZ-SCL quality system, shall be retained in a suitable environment.
2.3.2   Details of WHO, WHAT and HOW are defined in XYZ-SCL written procedures and job instructions.

3   **PURCHASING**

3.1   **General**

3.1.1   A purchase requisition, containing all relevant information and validated by an authorized person, shall be issued prior to any purchasing activity taking place.

3.2   **Assessment of supply sources**

3.2.1   Sources selected by the purchasing department for procurement of materials and/or services shall be evaluated and approved by the appropriate department and the quality manager prior to including them on a list of acceptable/approved suppliers.

3.2.2   Whenever possible, a minimum of three acceptable/approved suppliers shall be required to submit bids and each bid shall be evaluated by the appropriate functions. The managing director shall be the final authority on which bidder shall receive a purchase order.

3.2.3   The supply of items and services shall be processed from acceptable/approved suppliers. Records shall be maintained to substantiate supplier quality performance.

3.2.4   The extent of control over the purchasing activity shall include subsequent quality audits and monitoring at a supplier's facility as required.

3.2.5   A current list of acceptable/approved suppliers for items and services shall be maintained by the purchasing department.

3.3   **Purchasing data**

3.3.1   Purchase orders shall be reviewed by the appropriate functions to ensure that all pertinent information relative to the item and/or services to be procured is listed and the sources of supply have all necessary data, including designation of appropriate quality requirements.

3.3.2   All purchase orders and associated reference data shall be available for review by the customer as required.

3.4   **Verification of purchased product**

3.4.1   The inspection function shall evaluate all purchase items where any of the following conditions apply:

(a) Inspection of quality characteristics cannot be verified during subsequent processing or would require destructive testing.

(b) Inspection is necessary to verify that specific processes, tests or inspections required of the supplier were adequately carried out.

(c) Inspection at any other point would destroy or require the replacement of costly packaging materials.

3.4.2   Amendments to a purchase order shall be processed in the same way as the original, with reference made to the original purchase order.

3.5   **Customer facilities**

3.5.1   When required, a customer shall be afforded the right to verify at source, or upon receipt, that purchased items conform to specified requirements. This right of access shall extend to a sub-contractor's facility to permit verification at source.

3.5.2   Details of WHO, WHAT and HOW are defined in XYZ-SCL written procedures and job instructions.

4   CONTROL OF NON-CONFORMING PRODUCT
4.1   Non-conforming items

4.1.1   Non-conforming items shall be identified and segregated to prevent unauthorized use, shipment or inclusion with conforming items.

4.1.2   Applicable repair or rework forms shall be completed which shall identify the item, the deviation or discrepancy and shall be forwarded to the applicable department for review. The item shall then be appropriately classified to meet one of the following criteria:

— rework to meet the specified requirements,

— accept with or without repair by concession,

— regrade for alternative application,

— scrap.

4.1.3   Non-conforming items received from suppliers shall be handled in the same manner as in clause 4.1.2 above.

4.1.4   Personnel responsible for dispositioning non-conforming items shall ascertain that the deviation or discrepancy is clearly described relative to its acceptance criteria.

4.1.5   Decision on sub-contractors' non-conforming items shall be subject to approval by XYZ-SCL and the customer's representative.

4.1.6   XYZ-SCL shall maintain objective evidence to substantiate that repaired and reworked items have been re-inspected or re-tested according to applicable procedures.

4.2   Non-conforming services

4.2.1   Non-conforming services shall be identified and documented. Corrective action shall be initiated to correct the condition and prevent recurrence.

4.2.2   Where non-conforming services result in the production of non-conforming goods the control of these goods shall be as described in clause 4.1.2.

4.2.3   Details of WHO, WHAT and HOW are defined in XYZ-SCL written procedures and job instructions.

5   **CORRECTIVE ACTION**
5.1   The responsibility and authority for initiating corrective action shall
         be defined.
5.2   When non-conforming products are identified, the cause of the
         discrepancy shall be investigated, corrective action taken and preven-
         tative measures initiated.
5.3   When corrective action is necessary, controls shall ensure that the
         specified corrective action has been undertaken and is effective.
5.4   A system shall be implemented to ensure that any changes to existing
         procedures are recorded.
5.5   All system activities, and the associated objective evidence of product
         conformance, shall be analysed to ensure that potential causes of non-
         conforming products are detected and eliminated.
5.6   In order to detect and eliminate potential causes of non-conforming
         products, a continuous analysis of service reports and customer
         complaints shall be implemented.
5.7   Details of WHO, WHAT and HOW are defined in XYZ-SCL written
         procedures and job instructions.

N.B. In the context of this outline the term 'product' refers to both items and
services.

6   **QUALITY RECORDS**

6.1   **General**

6.1.1   Legible records shall be generated and maintained to support and substantiate all quality-related activities. These records shall provide evidence of the quality of the item or service and testify directly or indirectly that the product is in compliance with contractual requirements.

6.1.2   Records shall be maintained for all applicable activities such as:

   (a) system and compliance audits
   (b) verifications performed in accordance with customer or company requirements
   (c) reliability of procurement sources
   (d) control of non-conforming product (items and services)
   (e) corrective action on repetitive discrepancies
   (f) tests, approvals and audits by agencies, prime contractors and other clients
   (g) certifications for approval of personnel and processes

6.1.3   Accumulated records shall be reviewed and evaluated by responsible personnel for the purpose of improving systems, records, etc.

6.1.4   Verification records shall identify the product (item or service), applicable requirements, verifications performed, date of verification, verification authority, result obtained and the feedback of corrective action generated by the records.

6.1.5   Quality records shall include analyses of data resulting from verification activities. Associated records shall demonstrate the use of these data for corrective action.

6.2   **Retention of records**

6.2.1   Records shall be retained for the period required by company, by legislation, or as specified by customer, whichever is the greatest.

6.2.2   Records shall be stored in a suitable environment to minimize deterioration or damage and to prevent loss.

6.2.3   Where required by contract, records shall be made available for evaluation by the customer or the customer's representative.

6.3   **Disposal of records**

6.3.1   A system for the disposal of records shall also be established.

6.3.2   Details of WHO, WHAT and HOW are defined in XYZ-SCL written procedures and job instructions.

7   INTERNAL QUALITY AUDITS

7.1   The quality manager shall establish, document and implement a programme for audits which shall evaluate objectively the adequacy of the company's quality management system.

7.2   The audit programme shall define:

— the functions, procedures and instructions to be audited,
— the personnel qualified to perform audits,
— the frequency of audits,
— the methods of reporting findings,
— the means for having corrective actions agreed upon and implemented.

7.3   Audits shall include an evaluation of:

— activities, processes, work areas, items and services being produced,
— quality practices, procedures and instructions,
— certification, documents and records.

7.4   Audits shall be carried out by appropriately trained and qualified personnel who are not directly responsible for the area being audited.

7.5   Audits shall be performed in accordance with documented audit procedures utilizing check-lists which identify essential characteristics.

7.6   Management responsible for the area audited shall review, agree and correct deficiencies revealed in the documented audit results and shall implement corrective action to prevent a recurrence of the deficiency.

7.7   All action taken to correct deficiencies shall be re-audited to verify compliance.

7.8   Details of WHO, WHAT and HOW are defined in XYZ-SCL written procedures and job instructions.

8   **TRAINING**

8.1   All functions that require acquired skills and which could be adversely affected by the lack of such skills shall be identified, categorized and documented.

8.2   Documented evidence of personnel competence shall be retained and, at regular intervals through review, examination or other means, an evaluation shall be undertaken to determine whether personnel carrying out such functions require additional training or experience to rectify any shortfall.

8.3   Training shall be undertaken utilizing in-house courses or by training schemes operated by recognized third-party organizations.

8.4   Satisfactory completion of training shall be demonstrated by methods such as:

— examination,
— testing,
— certification,
— letter of attendance.

8.5   All records of competence shall be maintained and related to the identified training needs.

8.6   Details of WHO, WHAT and HOW are defined in XYZ-SCL written procedures and job instructions.

Appendix B
Typical procedure for the development of activity documents

Document Number

XYZ-DOC-002

Document Title

PROCEDURES — PREPARATION, STYLE AND FORMAT

Cover Page/Revision Status

REV	DATE	STATUS	BY	APPROVED
0	18.7.90	For comment		
1	20.8.90	Issued for use		

Page 1 of 5

CONTENTS

1.0 PURPOSE

2.0 SCOPE

3.0 REFERENCES

4.0 DEFINITIONS

5.0 ACTIONS

    5.1 Authorization to proceed
    5.2 Procedure format
    5.3 Procedure content
    5.4 Variations

6.0 DOCUMENTATION

1.0 PURPOSE

1.1 The purpose of this procedure is to describe the method of preparation, style and format of all procedures established for use by all departments and/or sections of the XYZ Services Company Limited (XYZ-SCL).
This procedure shall be used as an example of such preparation, style and format.

2.0 SCOPE

2.1 This procedure shall apply to all documents which identify the activities and functions of XYZ-SCL and shall be observed by all departments and sections without exception.

3.0 REFERENCES

3.1 XYZ-DOC-001 Numbering system for XYZ-SCL documents.

3.2 XYZ-DOC-003 Procedure for development, approval and implementation of activity documents.

3.3 XYZ-DOC-004 Procedures register.

4.0 DEFINITIONS

4.1 **Procedure** — A document that details the purpose and scope of an activity and specifies how and by whom it is to be properly carried out.

5.0 ACTIONS

5.1 **Authorization to proceed** — The need for a procedure shall be identified by the department or discipline manager concerned and the development of such agreed with the appropriate discipline head (refer XYZ-DOC-003).

5.1.1 Once the requirement has been agreed and an author delegated, the author shall obtain a definitive procedure number from the document control centre (refer XYZ-DOC-001). This procedure number shall be unique for the procedure to which it is to be applied and shall not be used to identify any other document. In the event that the decision to proceed with the procedure is rescinded, then the document control centre shall be so advised and the number reinstated for future use.

5.2 Procedure format

5.2.1 The cover page of the procedure shall be in accordance with form DOC-0021 (see attachment 6.1) and completed with the following information:

— document number,
— document title,
— cover page/revision status,
— revision and approval box.

Refer to the cover page of this procedure for standard format. The cover page shall always be identified as Page 1 of —.

5.2.2 The procedure's contents list shall always appear as Page 2 of —.

5.2.3 The contents page and all subsequent pages of the procedure shall be completed using XYZ-SCL standard bordered stationery (see attachment 6.2). Each page shall be identified by number and shall carry the appropriate document identification and revision in the bottom right-hand corner.

5.3 Procedure content

All procedures shall carry the same content which shall be as follows:

5.3.1 **Purpose** — which outlines the objective or intention of the document.

XYZ-DOC-002
Rev 1

5.3.2 **Scope** — which outlines the limits of applicability of the document, i.e. by whom it is to be applied

   5.3.3 **References** — which details other documents that have a bearing on the activities within the procedure.

5.3.4 **Definitions** — which explains words or actions not generally understood, or which may have a specific interpretation within the procedure.

5.3.5 **Actions** — which details the actions of those personnel involved in the activity. This section shall identify who does what and also how, when, where and why the activity is carried out.

5.3.6 **Documentation** — which lists any documentation necessary to implement the procedure. Samples of such documentation shall be attached.

5.4 **Variations**

5.4.1 The procedure's index shall always include the content as detailed in clause 5.3 above (see attachment 6.3). There shall be no variation. In the event that, for example, there are no references or definitions, then under the applicable heading the word NONE shall be inserted.

5.4.2 In the event that additional details are required to be incorporated as a supplement to the procedure, then these shall be incorporated as an appendix to the procedure.

6.0 DOCUMENTATION

6.1 Procedure cover page (DOC0021).

6.2 XYZ Services Company Limited standard border stationery (DOC0022).

6.3 Procedure contents page (DOC0023).

XYZ-DOC-002
Rev 1

Document Number

— — — — — — — — — — —

Document Title

— — — — — — — — — — — — — — — — — —

Cover Page/Revision Status

REV	DATE	STATUS	BY	APPROVED

Form No. DOC0022

CONTENTS

1.0 PURPOSE

2.0 SCOPE

3.0 REFERENCES

4.0 DEFINITIONS

5.0 ACTIONS

6.0 DOCUMENTATION

Appendix C
Glossary of terms

Unless otherwise indicated the definitions are as given in the International Standard ISO 8402-1986 (Quality-vocabulary).

Audit check-list: A document which guides the continuity and depth of an audit. (Author)

Corrective action request: A document which addresses a non-conformance to a system element, procedure or job instruction. (Author)

Customer: This term applies in both the internal and external sense and means the recipient of an item or service. (Author)

Job instruction: A document which directs personnel in a specific task.(Author)

Non-conformance: The non-fulfilment of specified requirements.

Organization: A company, firm, enterprise or association, or part thereof, whether incorporated or not, public or private, that has its own function(s) and administration. (Australian Standard DR 89201:R).

Procedure: A document which describes what is to be done and by whom, and how, when, where and why an activity is to be carried out. (Author)

Product (1): The result of activities or processes (tangible product; intangible product, such as a service, a computer program, a design, directions for use); or an activity or process (such as the provision of a service or the execution of a production process).

Product (2): The result of one's own endeavours. (Author)

Quality: The totality of features and characteristics of a product or service that bear upon its ability to satisfy stated or implied needs.

Quality audit: A systematic and independent examination to determine whether quality activities and related results comply with planned arrangements and whether these arrangements are implemented effectively and are suitable to achieve objectives.

Quality management: That aspect of overall management function that determines and implements the quality policy.

Quality manual: A document which describes, in general terms, the quality policies, procedures and practices of an organization. (Author)

Quality policy: The overall quality intentions and direction of an organization as regards quality, as formally expressed by top management.

Quality system: The organizational structure, responsibilities, procedures and resources for implementing quality management.

Quality system element: The administrative activities affecting quality that need to be implemented and controlled to ensure that the product or service meets specified requirements. (Australian Standard 2990-1987).

Quality system review: A formal evaluation by top management of the status and adequacy of the quality system in relation to quality policy and new objectives resulting from changing circumstances.

Bibliography

STANDARDS

ISO 8402-1986 Quality — Vocabulary.
ISO 9000-1987 Quality management and quality assurance standards — Guidelines for selection and use.
ISO 9001-1987 Quality systems — Model for quality assurance in design/development, production, installation and servicing.
ISO 9004-1987 Quality management and quality system elements — Guidelines.
ISO 10011 Generic guidelines for auditing quality systems.

Published by the International Organization for Standardization, Geneva.

AS 2561-1982 Guide to the determination of quality costs.

Published by Standards Australia, North Sydney.

BOOKS AND PUBLICATIONS

Barra, R. (1983) *Putting quality circles to work*, New York: McGraw-Hill Book Company.
Crosby, P. B. (1979) *Quality is free, New York*: McGraw-Hill Book Company.
Crosby, P. B. (1984) *Quality without tears*, New York: McGraw-Hill Book Company.
Department of Trade and Industry *Total quality management — A practical approach*, London: Her Majesty's Stationery Office.
Department of Trade and Industry *Quality management: A guide for chief executives*, London: Her Majesty's Stationery Office.

Department of Trade and Industry *Quality circles*, London: Her Majesty's Stationery Office.

Hutchins, D. (1985) *The quality circle handbook*, London: Pitman Publishing Limited.

Juran, J. M. (1964) *Managerial breakthrough*, New York: McGraw-Hill Book Company.

Mohr, W. and Mohr. H. (1983) *Quality circles: changing images of people at work*, Reading, Mass.: Addison Wesley.

Moir, P. W. (1988) *Profit by quality*, Chichester: Ellis Horwood Limited.

NSQC (1985) *Circle programme guidelines*, London: National Society of Quality Circles.

Oakland, J. S. (1989) *Total quality management*, Oxford: Heinemann.

Peters, T. J. and Waterman, R. H. (1982) *In search of excellence*, New York: Harper and Row.

Robson, M. (1982) *Quality circles: A practical guide*, Aldershot: Gower Publishing Company.

Sayle, A. J. (1988) *Management audits*, second edition, London: McGraw-Hill Book Company.

Stebbing, L. E. (1989) *Quality assurance: the route to efficiency and competitiveness*, second edition, Chichester: Ellis Horwood Limited.

Index

ELLIS HORWOOD SERIES IN
APPLIED SCIENCE AND INDUSTRIAL TECHNOLOGY

Series Editor: Dr D. H. SHARP, OBE, former General Secretary, Society of Chemical Industry; formerly General Secretary, Institution of Chemical Engineers; and former Technical Director, Confederation of British Industry.

MECHANICS OF WOOL STRUCTURES
R. POSTLE, University of New South Wales, Sydney, Australia, G. A. CARNABY, Wool Research Organization of New Zealand, Lincoln, New Zealand, and S. de JONG, CSIRO, New South Wales, Australia

MICROCOMPUTERS IN THE PROCESS INDUSTRY
E. R. ROBINSON, Head of Chemical Engineering, North East London Polytechnic

BIOPROTEIN MANUFACTURE: A Critical Assessment
D. H. SHARP, OBE, former General Secretary, Society of Chemical Industry; formerly General Secretary, Institution of Chemical Engineers; and former Technical Director, Confederation of British Industry

QUALITY ASSURANCE: The Route to Efficiency and Competitiveness, Second Edition
L. STEBBING, Quality Management Consultant

QUALITY MANAGEMENT IN THE SERVICE INDUSTRY
L. STEBBING, Quality Management Consultant

INDUSTRIAL CHEMISTRY: Volumes 1 and 2
E. STOCCHI, Milan, with additions by K. A. K. LOTT and E. L. SHORT, Brunel

REFRACTORIES TECHNOLOGY
C. STOREY, Consultant, Durham; former General Manager, Refractories, British Steel Corporation

COATINGS AND SURFACE TREATMENT FOR CORROSION AND WEAR RESISTANCE
K. N. STRAFFORD and P. K. DATTA, School of Material Engineering, Newcastle upon Tyne Polytechnic, and C. G. GOOGAN, Global Corrosion Consultants Limited, Telford

MODERN BATTERY TECHNOLOGY
C. D. S. TUCK, Alcan International Ltd, Oxon

FIRE AND EXPLOSION PROTECTION: A System Approach
D. TUHTAR, Institute of Fire and Explosion Protection, Yugoslavia

PERFUMERY TECHNOLOGY 2nd Edition
F. V. WELLS, Consultant Perfumer and former Editor of *Soap, Perfumery and Cosmetics,* and M. BILLOT, former Chief Perfumer to Houbigant-Cheramy, Paris, Président d'Honneur de la Société Technique des Parfumeurs de la France

THE MANUFACTURE OF SOAPS, OTHER DETERGENTS AND GLYCERINE
E. WOOLLATT, Consultant, formerly Unilever plc